eBook Edition first published in Great Britain in 2018 by
Blue Tao Publishing

ISBN 978-1-912872-04-6

Created with Vellum

THE LIGHTHOUSE KEEPERS

AN INSPIRATIONAL JOURNEY OF SELF BELIEF AND LOVE

GRAHAME ANDERSON

BLUE TAO

CONTENTS

Introduction vii

PART I
PRESENT DAY

1. The Concert 3
2. A Visit to Scotland 17
3. An Invitation 24
4. Family Reunion 31

PART II
THE EARLY YEARS

5. The Lie 45
6. The Headmaster 55
7. Good News 62
8. First Journey 67
9. Castle Toward 73
10. Average Amongst Peers 76
11. First Lesson 79
12. Lily 85
13. The Tease 91
14. The Assessment 94
15. On The Beach 99
16. A Visit to the Lighthouse 103
17. The Journey Home 120

PART III
PRESENT DAY

18. The Return 133
19. Dinner and Dance 139
20. Catching Some Light 142
21. The Night Sky 157
22. Finding Lily 160

A little bit of help 181
About the Author 183
Thanks 185
The Best Seat in the Universe 187

INTRODUCTION

Alfonso Mienstroff

My position as music critic is well documented. And yet after forty years of listening to private performances, something extraordinary has happened to me which I'm convinced words will never explain. I'm left feeling stripped of all emotion, maybe even my sanity, as my life has changed irrevocably. Everything I thought I knew about music has been turned on its head because of the performance I witnessed today. This has left me in a state of inner chaos.

Today, I listened to Max Bruford's *The Lighthouse Keepers*. His music and performance left me in a state of nothingness. His symphony, composed at the tender age of fourteen, is a work of musical genius.

To help you understand why I say this, you first have to know where I've been.

I've sat front row for most of the top celebrated concerts. I've interviewed every world-class musician that fellow critics could only ever dream of meeting. More importantly, I'm loved and hated by them all, depending on the individual critiques I have written.

I had been thinking there were no real greats left to hear. And yet, listening today to Max Bruford and his New World Symphonic Orchestra showed me there was a different level of music I'd never ventured into. It was so profound, every nerve ending in my being felt blunted, leaving me naked with little left to identify my battered soul.

Is such a thing possible on the mere hearing of a new piece of music?

Until today, I would have said no. But now, through first-hand experience, I am utterly convinced there are levels of music unknown or experienced by most.

It's strange, because many years ago, a dear friend of mine and fellow critic heard what he called 'a sound like no other' while listening to a string quartet. He described it as almost accidental, as the performers seemed unaware of what they had played. An unearthly vibration surrounded him, and he described the encounter as 'sitting at the feet of God.'

My friend was never the same again. He dedicated the rest of his life in search of hearing that sound once more. He became a man obsessed, similar to the addict seeking to recreate his first high.

Unfortunately, it was never to be. He was forever grateful he experienced it, and yet his soul was tormented. He said one thing to me before he died: that the noise he heard that day was 'more beautiful than music itself.'

That description haunted me for many years as I wondered if a sound 'more beautiful than music' could exist. If any person other than my dear friend had told me of this happening, I would have disowned it immediately. But he was no fool and I trusted him implicitly. If he said this sound existed, then I had no reason to doubt him.

I, too, wanted to experience something as beautiful as he had described. But after years of searching and being alert to the possibility, I accepted my quest proved futile.

And so I moved on.

Until today.

I was lost in the performance of 'The Lighthouse Keepers' when it happened to me. I heard it, or to be more explicit, I felt it.

Bruford's symphony affected me like no other music ever has. If I'm completely honest, it tore me apart emotionally and spiritually. And somewhere in the depths of the fourth movement, 'The Emptiness Within', this sound overwhelmed me.

Time stood still, as I tried with all my skill and experience to work out what was happening.

It wasn't the gentle melody that sat within the movement; it was violent and brutal and shook my being to its core. I tried to attune to the euphoria yet could neither recognise nor comprehend this sound and how it was compiled. I was gone, lost in the beauty of it. I knew from my late friend's description what had happened to me, but the sound was gone before I knew it and the movement played to the end as if nothing had happened. But I knew it had happened. I not only heard it, I experienced it in its totality.

As the orchestra played on, the four movements wound their way to the depths of my soul, leaving me to question everything that is my life.

Earlier in the day I had interviewed Max, who is humble and understated, which I welcomed dearly in this musical world of temperamental divas and narcissists. He revealed to me how he created his symphony at a music retreat in Scotland.

The first movement, 'Reaching New Lands', he wrote when he left England for the first time. The second movement, 'First Love', needs no explanation for those who remember who first stole their heart. This haunting melody pulls you deeper into a journey of love, where life's golden thread of happiness is inextricably entwined with its equal and opposite thread of sadness.

The third movement Max wrote after visiting a lighthouse. It was at this now famous lighthouse that he met the keepers, an old man and woman who were more than a touch eccentric. He said it was they who inspired him to write his symphony and the name of its third movement: 'The Lighthouse Keepers'.

The fourth movement and finale, 'The Emptiness Within', carries the listener close to the edge of a great abyss, bringing a new dawning and realisation. It's too late for the listener to realise what's happening, as the music plunges them to inner depths only ever reached by a precious few. You have to have faith that you will return from those depths, and I don't believe anyone who hears this will come out unscathed. I have no doubt listening to this symphony will change you.

The Lighthouse Keepers, culminating in 'The Emptiness Within', challenges everything you've ever known about your relationship with music. It will penetrate your spiritual being before merging with your soul. Hopefully, you'll experience what I did, which was far greater and beyond the simple chemical stimulus of the brain.

Allow your heart to surrender to this music. It will enter and permeate your soul, and only then will you feel the emptiness at the core of your being. Be patient and alert, be a witness to your self as these feelings of nothingness turn slowly to euphoria.

After experiencing this performance, I had grave doubts whether Max Bruford could have composed such a masterpiece as a mere boy. I foolishly believed this music had to have come from the experience of a master musician, my argument being it was too significant for one so young. And yet, on reflection, I'm now convinced a master musician would probably have complicated each part.

The Lighthouse Keepers was born from innocence. Pure, raw and unadulterated, flowing from the soul of this boy to his violin. He didn't try to interpret, challenge or improve upon it. He accepted what he could see and captured this music in its pure form, from some vast untapped source.

As I finish this review a word of warning, music lovers. When listening to this symphony, you'll believe you've reached the very depths of your soul, but you won't have. Try and delve deeper with this music, as far into the darkness as you can. Somewhere in there, you will discover yourself. It will be uncomfortable, even painful, but try and stay with it until every raw emotion you've ever owned is laid bare before you. Only then will you have reached a place where you can truly see yourself. Accept yourself as you are: your brilliance and your flaws. Recognise the beauty in sadness and embrace it before climbing back up to where love lives, in abundance. It is here you can fill your heart and then maybe you will understand yourself.

This, my friends, is what I heard from this music. It changed my life and I'm sure it will change yours.

Alfonso Mienstroff

I

PRESENT DAY

1

THE CONCERT

'More!'

Behind the heavy curtain, Max Bruford waited backstage at the Royal Albert Hall. A deafening chorus arose from the audience, impatient for him to return to the stage for the second half of the evening's performance. The chanting reached a crescendo, as did the excitement within the auditorium. He was exhausted and exhilarated, having just played one and a half hours. Going back onstage would sap every last ounce of his energy.

He stepped forward, but the stage manager blocked his path with an outstretched arm, signalling to let the audience wait another thirty seconds. Max counted down the seconds, listening to the audience getting louder.

The stage manager gave him the thumbs up and he took a deep breath and pushed through the gap in the curtains. As he made his way to the front of the stage, a spotlight momentarily blinded him. The crowd rose to their feet, ecstatic at his return. Max raised his arms and bowed to each side of the audience.

The volume from five thousand pairs of stamping feet thundered towards him. He was overwhelmed. He knew what he was about to play was what the crowd had waited four years to hear, his magnum opus.

He let the crowd have their moment and waved his violin bow, enjoying the reception. It had taken him a long time to accept praise. He remembered how this reaction used to make him feel embarrassed. Older now, he'd learnt to accept and enjoy the experience as much for the audience as for himself.

Raising his arms, Max hushed the crowd. Row by row they sat like an inverted Mexican wave. He signalled to them to settle down and bowed to the orchestra and choir, who had performed wonderfully tonight.

Max then nodded to the conductor, Hans Demonte, who stood, waiting to play the finale. Hans had handpicked each performer and Max relished having such a talent collective coming together to play his music. This must be at least the tenth time he had collaborated with Hans. As a conductor, Hans was the best; as a friend, Max avoided him because of his mood swings.

As Hans raised his baton, the words of the critic, Alfonso Mienstroff, floated through Max's mind. Earlier that week, Mienstroff had written *The Lighthouse Keepers* was 'an intricate musical tapestry, woven from the soul of God.'

First Movement – Reaching New Lands

Max struck his bow hard against the strings with a ferocity few musicians could achieve. The orchestra came racing in behind him, surrounding him in a wall of sound. Duelling musicians complemented each other as the string section fought hard against Max. He cut through, his violin racing over the top as the orchestra quietened into the background, leaving his melody suspended in mid-air. The strings danced while the harpist swept her hands over and over, creating a swirling effect around the theatre. Max hoped the audience would experience his music the way he intended.

As the orchestra settled into the rhythm of 'Reaching New Lands,' the tempo progressed to a tantalising, foot-tapping pace, daring the audience to get to their feet. The crowd were out of their seats for the few minutes it lasted.

Max turned to the orchestra and signalled to Hans, who brought the pace back down to a long, slow, lilting movement. The music grew louder, swaying back and forth as Max introduced his melody of the waves rolling back and forth, the orchestra in their long black evening wear flowing and moving in time as they played, mimicking the movement of the River Clyde, the stormy body of water in Scotland Max once travelled as a boy.

As he cast his mind back, he could see the water become choppy and changed tempo to that of a sea shanty. Darkness fell like a curtain over the auditorium, the faces in the crowd disappearing one by one until there was nothing left.

Max had experienced this phenomenon many times before during his performances. He ignored it and kept playing, feeling slightly nervous, even though he knew what was coming.

Across the full width of the theatre, the river in Scotland appeared before him, looking exactly as it did when he first wrote this movement. Dark and foreboding, he watched it rise and fall while tossing the ferry he stood upon. The stage felt as if it were moving with its force, the musicians present at the edge of stormy waters facing danger ahead.

He watched the scene before him, the waves crashing over the bow of the ferry and flooding the deck, the water rushing towards his feet.

Max closed his eyes as the music flowed through him. It was comforting being at one with the waves. Softly, the swell dropped, leaving behind a calmness. As he looked out into the darkness, a single ripple appeared. He followed it as it made its way across the theatre.

The orchestra was barely audible behind him, playing at a whisper. Only a solitary marimba could be heard, repeating a pattern like raindrops dripping into a pond and fading out to close the first movement.

Second Movement – First Love

Max surfaced, relieved, from the unique place his music had taken him to. The darkness was gone, and the audience were in front of him again. He prepared himself for the second movement, 'First Love'.

The movement began playfully with an oboe chasing a flute with bright, staccato phrases. The flute responded in short bursts, their tones intermingling with the higher pitches of a xylophone. Images of butterflies, flitting from flower to flower in search of nectar came to Max as he played. The introduction faded, leaving only him and the lead cellist playing the main theme.

As he played, he felt himself fall back, deep into the music again. He wanted so much to resist, but the chance to relive his memories drew him in again as both a reluctant and willing participant. Just to see her again, one last smile, her laughter and playfulness. He knew it would be difficult, but the chance would be worth every painful moment to see her for perhaps the final time.

It was a challenge not to break down as he played his heart out. The repeating melody brought him back to his meditative state and to his first love. The audience faded to darkness again as he teased Lily's melody out from the core of his violin. Her song was forever a part of his instrument.

Peering into the darkness, Max saw the campfire ablaze on the beach. He knew he was playing with the orchestra but felt distant from them. A couple danced around the fire, barefoot in the sand, moving in perfect rhythmic unison to his music. They came towards him, their bodies holding artistic lines the way only dancers can. He watched as they tangoed, their movements strict and sharp, yet fluid.

He saw Lily and himself through the darkness. She was, as ever, playful, her mischievous grin and then her laughter as she threw her head back, her neck beautifully lit by the firelight. Her eyes sparkled as she played games with him. The melody observed every detail. Her hair and how it covered her face. How she pushed a strand back behind her ear. Her lips soft and pink, curled in an innocent smile while all the time she teased him. Every tiny crevice of her lips, the wetness, all magnified as Max focused closer in. He wanted to reach forward and kiss her.

They mirrored each other's movements. His own image faded, leaving Lily's face taking up the whole of the darkness; his playing was hypnotic, not coming from any script. He was sure he could feel her breath on his face, warm and sweet. Her eyes locked with his and the moments of shared love came back to him. He was back with her: every touch, every caress, the smell of her perfume, her blue jeans and cheesecloth shirt, her hair soft against his face. He lifted his bow and waved to her; she smiled and returned by blowing him a kiss. It felt real, like that first time he remembered so well. It was magical: the first touch of their tongues, so warm and wet, the softest of kisses he would never forget.

He tried to control his emotions, but couldn't. Tears slowly dripped from his cheeks as he finished playing; his love of yesterday had disappeared into the darkness again.

She was gone.

Max felt empty.

The orchestra came back into focus and he could hear his melody building again.

He wasn't sure he could summon the courage to play this movement ever again. The pain ripped at his heart more severely each time he ventured there. The audience could see his tears and connected with him emotionally: they knew this was the reason he hadn't played his beloved tune for four years.

Taking charge of himself, Max changed pace for the final time to bring the movement to an end. He was immersed so deeply in his work he hadn't noticed the audience reappear.

A beam swept across the stage, illuminating the faces of the audience in front of him. He knew this was no stage spotlight.

Third Movement – The Lighthouse Keepers

The orchestra opened the third movement, allowing Max some breathing time. The timpani rumbled in the background, sending thunder rolling around the theatre.

And then silence.

A single note rang out, long and low from the baritone sax, the sound of the foghorn. It blew again, fell silent and repeated.

Once more the horn blew.

The audience sat still, some forgetting to breathe out.

Max looked up to see a thick fog rolling in over the top of the audience. His eyes searched for any movement. A pinprick of light pierced through, willing him forward. He watched as it swept past. This was no theatre spotlight, but the beam from a lighthouse.

The dark, foreboding shape of the lighthouse appeared through the fog, towering over the stage. High above from where Max stood, the beam circled. Slowly, the fog cleared, revealing a night sky lit by a thousand stars.

The foghorn fell silent.

The lighthouse dominated the theatre. Two figures looked down from the top. Max was transfixed as light came sweeping across the orchestra and choir, then out over the audience.

Flutes led the haunting Lighthouse melody, introducing a sense of danger. The woodwind section, ever steady, was building in the background. Max felt the players' energy as their harmonics melded with the choir's heavenly chorus. Without warning the brass section struck, bringing a sharpness to the auditorium. The strings and woodwind sections grappled with each other like some medieval jousting competition. Soprano voices resonated like angels rising with the power of the light, while the baritones brought darkness and danger from the depths with a menacing chant.

Max's violin soared ever upwards, matching the sopranos note for note. Coloured lights fired off above the audience from the distant stars and he watched as they streamed towards him, reflecting from distant planets, before coming to rest by the two mysterious figures atop the lighthouse. The orchestra settled deep into a repetitive sequence. Max cut through their mantra with his solo, lifting the spirit of everyone present as the night sky filled the dome of the Royal Albert Hall.

His stance changed, and he let his bow hang by his side. His body swayed to the melancholic melody building from the cellos. The sounds were begging him forward, towards the fourth movement, 'The Emptiness Within'. He desperately wanted to go there, and yet he felt frightened to do so.

Caught out by his own composition, he looked to the orchestra for help. Hans waved his baton, raising the tempo.

Max stood, unmoving. His gaze was fixed on the lighthouse, as it circled from dark to light. The beam slowed to a stop and settled on him, his body illuminated. He believed in its power. His senses trembled to the same vibrations as the music. Every cell of his being tingled, announcing to him he was alive. Finally, the light moved on.

Re-energised, Max faced the orchestra and nodded. It was his turn to take them to a place they may only have dreamt of, somewhere far beyond the comfort zone of their own musicianship. He had to lead them towards greatness, help them take the necessary leaps of faith. Their fear was what usually held them back.

He guided them to a lilting middle section. Almost in slow motion, the sound resonated around the hall and came straight back at him.

Max played an intricate pizzicato, fingers dancing up and down the fingerboard, note perfect. The audience followed, knowing every note by heart. The virtuosos in the crowd, and there were many, scrutinised his every move. These were the few who really understood the complexity of this master musician's ability. They often referred to his ability as intuition, sparring with intellect, to delight the initiated.

Max fell back to the slow, repetitive melody, his body

once more moving with the sway of the music. The orchestra followed, slowing down, into line, to match him note for note. It was a perfect union, a hypnotic repetition, repeating over and over. This rhythm took the audience closer towards meditation. It reminded Max of the chanting of Buddhist monks when aligning themselves with nature.

A true state of wonder happens rarely in one's lifetime. Max knew he could deliver it and that the audience would be confused as to what had happened to them, but they would think back on it over many years, trying to understand what it was they experienced. With the mantra playing over and over, their mind state was now in a similar place to where an enlightened master would place himself for meditation. Max wanted to give his listeners the same experience: overwhelming feelings of peace and love and, most importantly, the feeling of coming home.

Behind him, the low rumble from the timpani felt like a train hurtling towards him. The thrill for Max was never to play *The Lighthouse Keepers* the same way twice. Each orchestra he worked with knew the individual parts of each movement. However, they were never allowed to practise the completed symphony.

Max had planned it this way with Hans to keep his masterpiece fluid. There was no place for musicians to be casual or relaxed, as he needed them to taste the fear as music should always be alive.

Max went off on a tangent and watched the fear in the eyes of the musicians. The audience stiffened at every stroke from the racing strings. Their sound surrounded Max, placing him into the centre of a tornado of music. The sounds swirled around him, their many colours and textures exciting him.

The brass sped up with the percussion hammering

faster and faster. Max entered at lightning speed, caressing and swashing his violin, lost in a cadenza of hope. He was moving closer to the highest of high notes.

Like an out of control demon, the frenzied orchestra played every note in perfect time with Max. From the background, the choir broke through, their voices the heavenly sound of angels. The audience gripped the arms of the theatre chairs tightly.

And then it happened. Without warning, the music stopped.

Max looked round in confusion. He could see Hans waving his arms, the orchestra playing and the choir singing, and yet there he stood, somewhere in the middle of this wall of silence.

Had he failed somehow? Yet Max knew instinctively everything was okay because of the warmth the silence was giving him. He spun round and could see himself playing, in full flight, in tune with the universe. He stepped back and watched himself as he mastered the violin and interacted with the orchestra: this was exciting and something he never got to see while deep in play.

What was happening to him? Had he died? Was this enlightenment?

He looked out into the crowd, who hadn't seemed to notice what had happened and remained transfixed by his performance. Then, throughout the rows of faces, one person was highlighted, staring straight at him. Alfonso Mienstroff. The critic raised his hand towards Max, who waved back. Were they both alert to some sound that no one else could hear, or was there such a thing as silence within the music?

The moment broke as quickly as it had arrived and Max fell back into his playing armed with this new knowledge.

The sound from the choir was spiritual; Max changed direction three times, testing both Hans and the orchestra's ability to use their intuition. At last, all the musicians fell into place, each playing the same melody. With a clash of cymbals, the third movement drew to a close.

The crowd breathed out. Knuckles white, they slowly released their grip on the armrests as the conductor took them towards a musical waterfall. The music faded to little more than a whisper.

Fourth Movement – The Emptiness Within

The fourth and final movement fell into a familiar rhythm as the harpist repeated her mantra from earlier. It reminded Max of the tinkling waltz that played on his mother's jewellery box when he was young. He used to watch the ballerina spin in the tiny mirror stuck to the red velvet lining. The clarinets melded with the harp and a hypnotic wave filtered through the audience beyond just their ears. This rhythmic repetition entered their minds, moving deep within their hearts, the choir's angelic harmonies bringing calmness.

Max knew what they were going through. Every time he listened to the harp playing this section he witnessed different parts of his life. His experiences, the heartbreak, his broken love and the profound sense of loss, and all traded for what? He could see the audience were living every emotion with him. Written from a position of purest love, the music carried it to all who heard it.

Max knew he had one last job to do as he came out from the spell of the harp. It was time to reach through to the souls of the audience and take them and his musicians beyond the notes. He considered them all willing prey, many of them perfectly aware of the boundaries they would soon cross. His music was both art and poetry in a different dimension.

He played his melancholic melody once again. As he played the same notes over and over, he felt like a musical hypnotist in complete control of all around him. He could make his audience do whatever he requested through the power of his music, and it was up to him to bring them with him, emotionally.

As the spotlight shone down on him, his memories took him back to the lighthouse keepers as they offered him fame. He saw himself, a young boy, holding a glass bottle filled with dazzling light. He inhaled it and was sure he could feel power racing through his body.

The spotlight moved off him.

Mournful cellos twisted at his core, and his heart felt the deep pain of loss. He glanced across the theatre. Black clouds churned towards him, enveloping him in dark fog, pulling him into a well of sadness. His pain was real. Each time he played this he wanted to die. Max cried openly as he played, overwhelmed with grief. His fingers found notes that didn't exist to most players.

There was Lily, her arms reaching out towards him, pleading with him. He had sold her out, for the price of fame. He saw himself walk towards the spotlight with his violin, never looking back. Lily's face faded into the darkness, tear-stained and distraught. The orchestra played through their own grief, everyone affected by this music. Max pushed them to stay within the mantra, taking them to a depth they have never been.

Walking forward into the abyss, Max knew no love existed within its depths.

Life was cruel. Spent, he was vulnerable and knew he

couldn't stay at the bottom of this deep well too long, the pain being unbearable. Each time he performed this movement, his understanding grew of what he had lost in his quest for success. Each time he went deeper, but this time it was a step too far. The audience also felt the pain, their emotions in tatters. Max couldn't let them suffer much longer. This view into the void, which every human being has, was difficult enough for him, having experienced it many times.

The conductor knew he had to help Max to come back up to the surface; this was deeper than either of them had ventured before. Hans felt himself succumbing to the pain and understood why Max had to revisit this nightmare every few years. He waved his baton to the orchestra to let the repetition go to lift the spirit of the music.

As he did so, Lily's face disappeared and the lighthouse came back to the fore. Max played his final run away from the sadness towards a bright, uplifting melody. He was in unison with the choir, the orchestra playing his central theme, elevating the mood. Together they ended the suite with everyone holding the last note for ten seconds. Hans kept his baton mid-height.

A deadly silence followed: an important four bars of silence Max had written into his music, a space for reflection. People remained still, eyes closed, some clutching their hearts. The majority had a hint of fear on their faces, not knowing what had moved them so much. At last, Max nodded to Hans, who dropped his baton and bowed.

The crowd leapt to their feet, their clapping and cheering a deafening roar to all those on stage.

Max waved his bow towards the conductor, orchestra and choir. The head of each section came forward and they all bowed together. Max accepted a bouquet of flowers.

Again, they took their bows time after time, each one deeply affected by the emotional journey.

The crowd continued to clap, they wanted more, but there was no more. Max was finished. He had triumphed once again, or had he? He looked to his peers, the virtuosos who filled the second and third rows. Many nodded and bowed to him; Alfonso Mienstroff gave him a victory salute.

The lighthouse still shines, he thought, as he took his final bow.

2

A VISIT TO SCOTLAND

Max stayed behind for the after-concert celebrations, mixing with many of the musicians and VIPs who had backstage access. Members of the orchestra and choir were still on a high, complimenting each other on their performances. Hans Demonte gave Max a glass of champagne. They clinked glasses.

"We did it again, Max, although you scared me this time. Don't take an audience that far if we ever play together again."

Max nodded, he knew what Hans was saying. However, he was glad it had worked out so well.

After an hour of signing autographs, Max said his goodbyes. His taxi had been waiting twenty minutes outside the venue with the meter running. He asked the driver to take him to Euston station. He reflected on how the week had ended and felt relieved: the night had finished on a high after as perfect a performance as he could have wished for.

At Euston the destination boards flicked through the names, and he waited patiently until his train to Glasgow

Central was listed for platform two. He purchased a coffee and biscuit and headed for the sleeper train.

Surprisingly, the sleeper carriage was more comfortable than expected, allowing him to sleep the whole journey until awakened by the guard informing him the dining car was now serving. Max gazed at the passing scenery as he ate his breakfast, his pot of tea delightfully light. He made a note to buy Assam instead of his usual English Breakfast when he returned home. In the distance, Glasgow loomed out of the greyness. The last time he passed through here had been more than forty years earlier.

So many questions in his head demanded an answer. Max was determined to find out more about the strange old couple who had haunted his thoughts for years.

Grabbing his bag, he stepped off onto the busy platform. Again he focused on the boards as he tried to find Gourock amongst sixteen different platforms. He spotted his train. It was the first three carriages leaving from platform fourteen in less than ten minutes. He ran. A few minutes later, he boarded the train. It pulled out of the station, heading to the small town on the west coast of Scotland where he would catch a ferry to Argyll.

Max had always found train journeys similar, no matter where he was in the world. There were the usual industrial buildings and graffiti that every city seemed to suffer from. Listening in on some passenger conversations, he found himself struggling to make sense of the accent, even although he had worked with many Scots over the years. Twenty minutes into the journey, the scenery changed dramatically to the landscapes he remembered.

As the countryside opened up with the Scottish mountains dominating the skyline, Max down glanced at his guidebook. The train was following the River Clyde.

According to his book, it was called a river but it was actually an inlet and part of the Atlantic Ocean. Max remembered its state could go from rough seas to glass pond in a matter of minutes. On the opposite side of the river, the hills of Loch Lomond loomed ominously. It was to this backdrop that he had written his first composition.

He pored over his guidebook while watching the route. Every landmark was steeped in history. If the author was accurate, it would seem the Scots changed the world in so many different fields of industry. They were incredibly inventive.

The train reached the end of the line and pulled into Gourock. With bag in hand, Max headed to the ferry terminal.

"No ferries today," said the ticket master, "the crews are on strike."

Max looked at the man in disbelief. Forty years he had waited to come back, and with only three days of leave, he had been stopped in his tracks because of a union strike.

"I have to get across the river. Does anyone have a small boat I could charter?"

"You don't know this area, do you?"

"Not very well, but I've been here before."

"No one would take you across on a small boat. There's no demand for such a service."

"Is there anything I can do? It's important I get across."

The man looked both ways then leaned in towards Max. "I'm not supposed to tell you this. Follow the coastline for two miles, keeping the water on your right hand side. There's another ferry service that will take you across. There's one every twenty minutes. But I never told you – it's our competition. You can get a taxi outside the station."

"Thanks, you're a lifesaver." Max pressed a couple of

pounds into the man's hand and headed out of the station. He decided to walk after having been sat on trains all night.

Setting his violin case on his back, Max appreciated the new rucksack-style instrument cases that left him hands-free. He tipped his suitcase onto its wheels and headed through the town centre. The ticket master had said to keep the river on the right.

Gourock was instantly likeable. The locals seemed friendly, and the main street was busy with small shops and thriving cafés. The names of the small boutique shops and bars fascinated him. Cleats, The Kempock, The Pirate and Bluebelle, Café Continental and Coorie Doon. He noted the names, planning to look up their meanings later, especially Coorie Doon. He was sure 'Doon' meant 'down' in the Scots language but he had never heard the word 'Coorie'. With no high street chains in sight, only one establishment was familiar to him, and that was the Post Office.

Through the gaps between the buildings, he could see the river with its striking backdrop of mountains and hills. The hills were every shade of green, blue and purple.

There was plentiful activity on the river with quite a few sailboats and kayaks. In the middle of the channel loomed something Max had never seen in real life: a nuclear submarine. This wasn't something he expected to see and he was surprised at the size of it, as it dwarfed the other vessels on the water. It was being guided by two tugboats while fast-moving RIBs, possibly military, patrolled up and down each side of the enormous black hull. Naval personnel stood along the deck, with two or three officers on the conning tower. The somewhat threatening vessel headed towards the opposite side of the river.

Max watched as the submarine disappeared from view into a sea loch. The topographical features of this area provided the perfect place to hide these underwater giants. He thought about writing a piece of music about them, the silent keepers of world peace. Max pulled out his notebook and flicked to his 'Ideas and Future Projects' section. He wrote one word: 'Polaris'.

He pushed on towards the ferry, passing the last of the houses on the shore side. The view opened up into a full panoramic vista of the river in all its splendour. He questioned himself on why he hadn't visited Scotland more often, knowing deep down he had the answer.

Something else caught his eye. Something he hadn't seen since the sixties: an outdoor swimming pool positioned next to the river. He marvelled at the swimmers and families seated around the pool on deck chairs and sun loungers. How could they could swim outdoors in what must have been temperatures of eight degrees? A stiff breeze was also coming off the river, hitting the swimmers standing in their soaking wet costumes. Max concluded these people were either very hardy or extremely brave in this climate.

He breathed deeply as the cold air filled his lungs. It felt good. There was something unique about Scotland's air. There was a sharpness to it unlike the heavy fuel-loaded scent that Londoners suffered every day. Where he lived, the traffic pollution and overpopulation had scuppered any chance of clean air. This air here was as pure as could be. The Scots could bottle this.

A ferry came into view halfway between the two land points. Painted bright red, it was stark against the blueness of the water. The ferry's car deck was filled with buses, cars and people all queued and ready to get off. Max upped his pace, his suitcase feeling far heavier now than when he started. He arrived just as the ferry docked. He recognised the boat; it was definitely the same style as the one he travelled on as a boy. As the vehicles trundled off, Max felt envious of the pedestrians and cyclists heading across the water with the ability to explore this magnificent wilderness.

Leaving his suitcase on the car deck, he headed upstairs to the balcony and watched as the cars manoeuvred into the narrow vehicle lanes.

The water was calm and flat, almost like glass. Cormorants stretched their wings, resting on the pillars of a once useful pier and catching what little heat there was from the sun. Ducks swam round the ferry, while fifty yards in front a seal popped its head out of the water, surveying its surroundings before submerging again without a ripple.

The vibration of the ferry changed as it moved off, leaving Gourock behind. Max was surprised at the shape of the ferry as it seemed to be square at the front. He thought all vessels had a bow to cut through the water but this ferry, square as it was, seemed to be managing fine. As it reached the midway point, its sister ferry passed with a toot of the horn. Max looked down the river and saw a number of islands completing the landscape.

The breeze cut through Max's clothing, bringing back thoughts of the brave swimmers standing poolside. The boat rocked and threw Max back in time. It was here he'd first heard his symphony as the motion of the boat carried him home. It wouldn't leave his head. It was his first composition, 'Reaching New Lands'. As it began to play in his thoughts, Max started to drift.

The boat bumped against the pier, returning him to the present moment. The ferry locked onto the pier. Forty years of waiting for this moment, and it had finally arrived.

He headed up the ramp to the waiting taxi.

"Where to?"

"The Seafront Hotel, Innellan."

The driver moved off without a word. Max looked at the houses and buildings as they drove. It troubled him that the driver hadn't spoken to him since he got into the car. No mention of how beautiful a day it was, nothing but a stony silence.

They passed through Dunoon then headed south towards Innellan. After fifteen minutes the driver stopped outside a pleasant-looking hotel with flower baskets hung along the walls. Max paid the driver and grabbed his case and instrument.

3

AN INVITATION

Max climbed the few steps to the hotel. It was a strange arrangement; he had to walk through the dining room and past the diners to the far end to reach the check-in area. People were eating lunch, with some drinking wine and coffee.

The manager checked Max in and showed him to his room. It was comfortable and clean, the best he could hope for, staying in a small village. Max placed his suitcase on top of an old wooden dresser and opened it. He decided he would leave his clothes in the case instead of unpacking it, considering the short time he would be here.

He was sure the water in Scotland would be perfect but he ran the cold water tap for a minute before filling the kettle. Old habits are hard to break. Rummaging through his bag, he fished out a lemon and ginger teabag. After years of travelling, he had adapted his ways when drinking tea, opting for flavours that didn't need milk. He'd had too many unfortunate experiences in hotels where there was either no milk, powdered milk or greasy milk that had turned from lying in the room too long. He picked up the *Dunoon*

Observer, the local paper left for him by the owner. "Let's see what exciting things happen here," he said out loud.

After flicking through the pages, Max concluded that the ferry strike was the main headline, the other items being community-based news: darts competitions; sheriff court; and births, marriages and deaths. *No murders*, Max thought. *It must be wonderful to live in a place where murder isn't common.*

He sat on a chair sipping his tea while watching the boats on the water. How fortunate the locals were to wake up to this view every morning compared with the craziness of London, where buses and taxis fought with gridlocked traffic and cyclists risked their lives weaving in and out through the gaps.

He noticed the houses were evenly spread along the road, the majority facing the river. The hotel was more restaurant with rooms than a hotel. He flipped through his local guidebook and decided he would dine in the restaurant after reading the reviews giving it nine out of ten stars. It was clear people travelled for miles to eat here. After an hour of violin practice, Max headed downstairs to secure his table for the evening before going to explore the area.

The architecture of the buildings was mainly Victorian with a few modern structures peppered in between. *The people who built these in the 1800s must have been reasonably affluent*, he thought. The roads were quiet, and the sun was trying, albeit unsuccessfully, to push some heat towards him. He headed up the hill to give his legs a workout against the steep gradient. He was badly in need of some exercise. The views from the higher streets were breathtaking, looking down onto the river. He scanned the panoramic view and watched a yacht race, wishing he could be crewing for one of the teams. A brown tourist sign pointed further up the hill to Knockamillie Castle. *A real castle in a village this size!* He followed the trail through the long grass, as birds flew low over his head. At first, he thought they were swallows, because of their speed, but they didn't move like swallows. He kept his eye trained on them as they were fluttered from side to side. *Bats*, he thought, *out feeding on the midges.* That was the only negative memory he had of Scotland: being attacked by thousands of midges. When visiting this area as a teenager he had explored the local pine forests a few times with the other students. Without warning, clouds of ferocious midges had descended upon them, forcing them to run in all directions. They weren't dangerous like mosquitoes, just irritating as for tiny insects they packed a big bite.

Max came across a pile of stones with a little staircase rising towards the sky. *So this is the famous Knockamillie Castle. There's not much of it left*, he thought. He took out his phone and photographed the castle remains.

After a while, he decided to head back down past some dog walkers. They said hello to him, which felt strange. He didn't reply feeling slightly embarrassed, but after a few other people greeted him he realised this was normal and so started to answer. In London it would be unusual for someone out walking to say hello, especially as dusk fell.

"Hello there, are you here for the party?" A loud Scottish accent announced the presence of two men.

"No, you must have me mixed up, I'm just visiting the area."

"Ah, I thought you were with the band. I saw you come into the hotel earlier with a violin case. At least, that's what it looked like."

"Yes, it is. I suppose as a stranger in a small village I must stick out."

"Not really, the village will be transformed tomorrow. We've over one hundred people coming together from all over the country tomorrow. They're coming to see this man and his family." He pointed to his companion.

A broad-looking man with a huge beard stretched out his hand. "G'day mate, the name's Colin McCartney. Pleased to meet you."

"Ah, Australian, welcome to England."

"England?" said the first man, "We're in Scotland."

"Oh sorry, I've just arrived from London, forgot where I was for a moment. Welcome to Scotland."

"Thanks, mate. I'm over visiting my cousin Luke here with our oldies. He's going to put us all up at his place for a few nights. They haven't been home to Scotland for over twenty-five years. The family have laid on a party in the village hall tomorrow. I got the short straw, I mean, the job of looking after them to make sure they arrived here safely."

"At least you got a trip to Scotland, get you away from all that sun."

"True. Although shepherding four seventy-year-olds around Scotland, London and Ireland for three weeks is a lot of organising."

"I bet. Rather you than me, Colin." Max winked.

"You're welcome to come along tomorrow, get a bit of tucker. It's free for all," Luke said.

"Sounds like it will be one to remember. Unfortunately, I'm busy retracing my own steps to Castle Toward and the lighthouse. I was here forty years ago so it looks like we're both on similar missions."

"Forty years ago. You don't look old enough," the Australian laughed. "Our oldies are jet-lagged having just flown from Sydney with no stopovers."

"I would love to go to Sydney," said Luke. "Been stuck here all my life, hardly been out of Scotland."

"One day, Luke. We just need to get you on a plane," said Colin.

"I've been to Sydney," said Max. "Fabulous place."

"Oh? Whereabouts did you visit?"

Max realised he hadn't really seen anything of Sydney. One of the disadvantages of travelling with an orchestra and a choir was the expense. To keep that number of people in hotels and food was costly, so concerts were stacked tightly together. He had been to Sydney six or seven times, and the most he'd seen was inside the Opera House and views of the bridge. It felt rather pathetic now he thought about it.

"Sydney Opera House, beautiful building, wonderful acoustics, a joy to visit."

"Aw yeah, love it. I've been to a few concerts there. Who did you go to see?" asked Colin.

"I didn't go to see anyone. I was playing. Well, not just me: I was part of an orchestra."

"Unbelievable, mate. What were you playing?"

"Violin."

"I think my cousin means who were you supporting?" said Luke. "Were you backing up an artist or was it a famous orchestra playing?"

Max scratched his head. It was awkward to explain he was the headline act without it sounding embarrassing. The majority of the public never recognised him unless they were classical fanatics. "I was the solo violinist. I had an orchestra backing me."

The two men looked at each other then back to Max.

"Jeez mate," said Colin. "You must be bloody good. What's your name?"

Please don't ask the embarrassing question, Max

thought. Any time he said his name no one ever knew who he was. "Max Bruford."

"Max Bruford, I know you," Luke's eyes lit up. "I've seen you on *Last Night of the Proms*. I know your work. They play you on the classical channel all the time."

Colin's mouth dropped open. "So are you, like, the Bruce Springsteen of the classical world? Are you famous?"

"Not something I would say about myself, but I'm reasonably well known."

"Don't let him talk himself down, Colin. This guy is super famous."

"Blimey, who'd have believed walking up a hill in Scotland, we'd meet a big star in the music world," Colin said. "Are you sure you can't make it to the village hall tomorrow and play us a couple of songs? The oldies won't believe us when we tell them we have a famous musician coming to play for them. That would give them summit to talk about when they get home. Would you do that for us?"

"I would love to, but unfortunately I've got another appointment. I'm only here for a flying visit."

"Fair enough, mate. If you don't ask, you don't get. Remember, you have an open invitation if you do change your mind. You can always join in with our ceilidh band if you want."

Max thanked the cousins for their offer. The three men had started to scratch as they stood talking. The midges were rife.

"I can't take these midges," Max said, rubbing his head. "I'm heading back to the hotel. It was nice meeting you. Enjoy your family gathering and safe trip back to Australia." He ran down the hill to the hotel and freshened up before heading to the dining room. It was crowded, no doubt due to the family gathering.

The staff in the hotel were well trained. Dinner was served to perfection, each course of a quality not usually delivered in such a small establishment. The meal would have cost a fortune in London. Max cleared his plate in all three courses, satisfied with the local fayre. He drank two glasses of red and watched the boats head back towards the marina directly opposite. The sky was ablaze as the sun sank behind the hills.

4

FAMILY REUNION

Max was up early and had finished his full Scottish breakfast before the other guests had visited the dining room. His breakfast was slightly different from what he would eat back home and he wasn't so sure about the potato scones, which he thought had a strange texture.

He decided he would visit both the castle and lighthouse if he had time, but before that he wanted to squeeze in a couple of hours of practice. He placed his mute onto the violin's bridge to reduce the sound significantly when he played and hopefully wouldn't annoy the other hotel guests. A new melody had invaded his head since he had woken and he wondered if it was something he had heard before, or whether it was his own creation. He took out his notepad and wrote down the music notation for the central theme. He wrote the date and place name, 'Innellan', to remind him of where he was when he started the tune.

Max felt fortunate to be able to compose on the move. Many of his contemporaries couldn't write unless they had silence or were in a particular place at a specific time.

He could write anywhere as long as he had his notebook and a pencil to hand. He had brought his first ever notebook with him on this journey, containing all his notes and feelings. He loved this battered old book, its pages dog-eared and tired looking. The original words on the cover had faded and the pages were separating from the spine, which was why he had to keep it together using a piece of elastic. As tired as his notebook looked, it brought him many fond memories of the early days when he started composing.

He browsed through the pages, revisiting the compositions he had written back then. There were some good pieces, but he knew he could do better now.

He smiled at some of his sketches placed between the words of songs and melodies. Big Ben was coming down the side of one page; small cottages, an elephant, and the lighthouse on others. The lighthouse was an image he had doodled into many of the spaces throughout his notebook. On one page it was sketched with seals on the rocks in front of it. On others, he had drawn it casting its beam of light out across the pages. He'd illustrated the old man and woman on a double-page spread, but it wasn't a fair likeness: his limitations in art was drawing people.

The hotel was busy, and the dining area filled up. People came in off the street for breakfast. An elderly couple asked Max if they could share his table. He nodded. It was probably time to go anyway, but he had just ordered a pot of tea.

The couple sat chatting to each other and then it happened, just as Max had predicted to himself. The first question to get him involved.

"Are you here for the family gathering?" the elderly woman asked.

Max smiled. This must have been the most significant event to happen in the village for a long time.

"No, I'm just visiting the area. I'm staying at the hotel for a few days."

The elderly gentleman spoke up. "Lucky you, son. We've got to make sure we get the last ferry home at midnight, or we'll be stuck here overnight. I talked to the manager of this hotel, in the event we miss the ferry, but he said they were fully booked. No room at the inn, if you get my meaning."

Max nodded. "I'm sure you'll catch your ferry. You can always sleep on my floor if you miss it." He smiled as he said it.

"Don't encourage him or you might end up having visitors," the woman said. "Once my Peter gets a good drink in him, he'll sleep anywhere. He doesn't care. Must be something to do with how he was raised, seven of them in one room and kitchen. All five kids sharing the one bed."

"Aye, that's how it was, Hannah. We didn't have much money, but we were close as a family could get."

"Consider yourselves lucky," said Max. "I was an only child. I always wanted to have a brother or sister."

"Oh dear," said the woman. "There's nothing better than a big family. That's why we're here today. My two sisters and their husbands have come over from Australia. We're going to give them a real shindig of a party they'll never forget."

"Aye, nobody can throw a party like us Scots," Peter agreed.

Max smiled again then finished his tea. "I hope you have a wonderful reunion. Enjoy seeing your family; I'm sure it will be very special."

In his room, he took out his violin and polished it with a

dry cloth, before tuning it. He played a pizzicato exercise to warm-up.

He took out his notebook and looked at the latest additions. He looked at the title – Innellan – and started to play his melody. He was pleased with it. He thought of the family he had met and their relatives travelling from Australia. He wondered how far the rest of the relatives had journeyed and if they came from every corner of the country. He played a few phrases and wrote an upbeat melody mimicking the family's excitement. From there he pictured them all coming together, the reunion. He composed a tune specifically for the sisters. Thinking of sisters, the world over, he knew it didn't matter how near or far they were: sisters are always sisters. They never lose sight of each other, even if all they have at times are memories. He decided to re-arrange this melody and use it to finish the end piece as they went their separate ways once more.

He flicked through his notebook and found a tune he had written years earlier. It had been for a large family celebration in Italy. He altered it to suit.

Lastly, he added a fun section. He imagined the old boy, Peter, crossing the dance floor with too many whiskies in him. He blended this with the only Australian tune he knew well. He played it through a few times and felt satisfied with how it had all come together. He made a mental note to compose like this more often. He made a couple of small changes and wrote it out clean on a new sheet, and titled it, 'Family Reunion'.

Max relaxed for a while, reading. He didn't have time these days to read full-length novels, having such a full diary. His preference was for small inspirational books filled with short stories. He heard a commotion outside and looked out across to the village hall. Cars were parked along the main road and onto the pier. Outside the building hung a large 'Welcome Home' banner. Balloons were tied to the railings and everywhere else possible. A solo piper played 'Scotland the Brave' on the bagpipes.

The Australians arrived and were being introduced to the family members lined up outside the hall. There were hugs, kisses and squeals as they met their family of yesteryear.

Max tried to imagine what it would be like to be part of something so beautiful. The closest he came to having a family was when touring with the orchestra, which always felt like family to him. He loved travelling with a large group where he could spend time with other artists and get to know them.

He made the decision to drop into the hall on his way out of the village. If they asked again, he would play his new tune for them.

He put on a small rucksack, picked up his violin and headed out.

As he approached the village hall, he could already hear music bouncing out the door. He stepped in and looked around. The place was busy. People said hello and welcomed him, thinking he was part of the family. Colin spotted him and made his way over to meet him.

"G'day, mate. You came. Thank you so much for coming. Can't believe it. Follow me, and we'll get you some food and the finest scotch."

"Honestly, I'm fine. I just popped in and thought I would play a couple of tunes for you."

Colin led Max to a table to meet his parents. He introduced them. Colin's father, Dave, and his brother, George, stood up to greet him and shake hands.

"Can't believe you are here," said Dave, taking a seat.

"We've seen you perform twice at the Opera House. Once in 1996 and the other in 2000 at the millennium concert."

"No. You've come to see me before? Thank you."

"Yes, we've all been fans for years."

"I remember playing the millennium concert. I loved it. All the boats in the harbour, decorated and lit up like big angelfish."

"Yeah, us Aussies know how to put on a show."

"You certainly do. I've had brilliant times down under."

George had a broad smile on his face. "You've made me a very happy man with *The Lighthouse Keepers*," he said. "It's been one of my favourites for the past thirty years. It's so emotional. Only a chosen few can write music like you do. I think you've been given a gift from the heavens."

"Thank you. I agree with you. I believe I was blessed as a child, Mr McCartney."

"George, call me George. Jeez, you Brits are too formal."

"Sorry, George. Did you know the lighthouse I wrote about is only a couple of miles from where we sit? Toward Lighthouse. That's the reason I'm here, retracing my steps. Just like your family. I'm heading there now for my own reunion."

"Really? I hope we can squeeze in a visit. Today we've got to do all the family stuff."

"I understand."

"Are you going to play us a tune while you are here? Would it be possible to play *The Lighthouse Keepers* for me?"

"I couldn't, I'm afraid, it needs the orchestra behind it to give the impact. A solo violin won't do that. But I'll play the main theme for a minute or two, if that's okay?"

George shook his hand. "If you play that you'll make our trip back home more special than you can imagine."

They ate some food and Max relented and had a whisky or two and then another few. The Scottish were very persuasive when it came to having a 'wee dram' and soon his head was feeling a bit woozy. He enjoyed celebrating with the family and didn't feel too out of place, as he could see many of them hadn't met each other before either. Assuming he was a long-lost cousin, many asked which branch of the family he was from.

The band, an acoustic/electric ensemble, played a selection of Scottish and modern songs. Max was dragged reluctantly onto the dance floor. Dancing was something he had never been comfortable with, but tonight he decided to let go and have fun. Dance after dance, partner after partner, he joined in to the fullest. Afterwards, he was exhausted especially after a few of the traditional Scottish dances.

Celebrating with this family reminded him how the strangest unforeseen circumstances were almost always the most memorable moments in his life.

Eventually, Colin stepped forward and took the microphone.

"Are you all enjoying yourselves?"

"Yes," a chorus of voices came back to him.

"As you know we're here to celebrate Sally, Dave, George and Isabel, coming home from Australia. It's been a long time coming and this I have to say is what they miss most: family."

The crowd were silent. It was an emotional speech. Colin walked the audience through how his parents and aunt and uncle had left Scotland, hoping to find a better life.

"Living in Australia is wonderful. There's no doubt about it, life seems better in the sun. But without the rest of our family there, it leaves an empty feeling inside. The oldies want me to thank everyone for giving up their time and making the effort to be here today. We know it's been a journey for you to get here and it's appreciated. Can I ask you to make sure every single one of you has your photo taken with us Scottish Aussies? We are having a scrapbook made about today to keep the memories alive, and we want everyone to be part of it. Including you, Max."

Everyone clapped. A few of the women and men wiped away tears. Max noticed Peter and Hannah sat holding the hands of their sisters, not wanting to let go. They wanted to enjoy every second being with them as it might be the last time they ever saw each other.

"Yes, that's right. We have a very special guest with us today. He came to us out of the darkness last night as we walked the high road. A chance meeting that will change all our lives for sure. This man is a legend in the world of classical music."

A few in the audience groaned.

"Less of that, you philistines. You may not know him by name, but you will have heard his music on TV and radio. Unbelievably, he has joined our family gathering and dropped in to help us celebrate. Please note, you will forever be able to claim you were at a private concert – not in Carnegie Hall where he usually plays, but in Innellan Village Hall – with none other than Max Bruford. Please put your hands together for our world-famous guest."

Everyone clapped and sat down at the tables arranged around the perimeter of the hall. Max walked to the microphone.

"Thank you, Colin, for such an eloquent introduction. When I say 'eloquent', I mean for an Aussie bloke. You managed to say a full sentence without mentioning beer or barbecue."

The audience laughed.

"I would like to thank Sally, Isabel, Dave and George for letting me gatecrash this family gathering. I knew no one when I came to this village yesterday, and now I feel I've inherited a ready-made family and one I would be proud to be part of."

Everyone clapped.

"Enough talking, let's play some music." Max took out his violin and checked its tuning. "Before I start I'll just give you a little background to this tune. I wrote it after meeting Luke and Colin last night and Peter and Hannah this morning. The tune starts with your family members setting sail to Australia. A new adventure for them all, but tinged with sadness at the loss of their family. As they build their lives in a faraway land, I bring in hope. They work hard to create a good standard of living to make their children proud and to prove the uprooting has been worth it. The next phase is of them missing out on family occasions like this and hoping for letters in the post. Finally, I finish with them coming home again, like they have today. Meeting family they've not seen for years, and younger nieces and nephews for the first time. I end the song with them heading back to Australia and the loss you all feel. I hope you like it; it's called *Family Reunion*."

Max picked up his violin and bowed to the Australians sitting at the top table. "Leaving Home," he announced into the microphone. Over and over he played his music until he could see the family well up, tears flowing, they were with him, moving with his music. He changed the rhythm into a more upbeat step and spoke again.

"Hope."

The band sitting at the side exchanged glances. As good as they were, they felt overwhelmed by this maestro driving the crowd with every note. The room was alive with delight. *Hope is working*, thought Max.

"Missing Family."

With that, Max returned to the repetitive refrain of broken hearts, before slowing down.

"Family Reunion."

The pace picked up and excitement and anticipation filled the room. Some members of the audience got up and danced. Max cut into a silly beat.

"Peter after too many whiskies."

Everyone laughed. The sound imitated a drunken man crossing a dance floor with notes slurring and pitch bending.

"Heading Home."

He spoke it quietly, but started to build an accelerating melody. As a last-minute addition, Max added the main theme from *The Lighthouse Keepers*. The Australians listened in awe, their hearts full. Max nodded to the band to join in. They didn't need to be asked twice and immediately they were on their feet playing behind Max, the accordion player matching his pace, the drummer playing a march on the snare drum as it built over and over. Max asked the singer to finish with a special tune they all could sing together.

The singer took the microphone. "Can everyone please get on the floor for Australia's unofficial national anthem."

Everyone in the hall stood up, and many went onto the dance floor.

"Everyone take hands, please?"

Max started slowly playing the melody of 'Waltzing Matilda', before the singer broke into song joined by George, and soon the rest of the family and the band, as the beat sped ever faster. Cousins Morag and Phil took to the floor and danced the Highland Fling. Phil had a hankie with knots tied at each corner balanced on his head and his trouser legs rolled up. A piper marched in, making his way round the hall playing the tune on his bagpipes, followed by a procession of children. The whole family sang the song over and over until the band finally slowed to a stop. Exhausted, the dancers made their way back to their seats to rapturous applause.

Back at the table, Max placed his violin into his case.

"Did you really compose that tune for us today?" Dave asked.

"I did, I wrote it this morning. It came quite easily."

"It was beautiful," said Sally. "You caught the emotion from leaving home, that's exactly how I felt. It all came rushing back."

"Me too," Isabel agreed. "That tune was the story of my life. Now I don't want to go home with all my family here. It's the most dreadful feeling having two countries to live in; you don't know where you want to be. Australia's where our kids consider home, so we have to be there for them, but Scotland is where we consider home. It's hard."

George shook Max's hand. "Tune of the day? 'Waltzing Matilda'."

Max smiled.

"I'm pulling your leg, Max. I worked in the shipyards and then in a garage, and I've never cried in my seventy years like I did when you played that song. Thank you. You need to record 'Family Reunion' on your next album."

"I think I will. But it's I who must thank you. Without your invitation, I would never have written that tune. It's still rough, but I'll refine it. Come and see me next year at the Opera House. I'll get you front row tickets."

"Free, I hope," said George with a twinkle in his eye.

"Of course. I'll invite you onstage."

"I was joking about the free! We'd love to come along, Max," said Dave. "Consider yourself an honorary member of the McCartney clan."

The men hugged, and Max left the hall after they had all posed for photographs. Thrilled with the wonderful reception to his new composition, Max returned to his hotel room to shower and rest. There he reflected on the infectious warmth of the family gathering and how natural it seemed to everyone there. He missed not being part of a large family.

The whisky was still affecting him and so he decided to lie on his bed for an hour's rest before heading off to the lighthouse and castle. As he began to drift off, he cast his mind back to the first time he'd heard the name Castle Toward.

II

THE EARLY YEARS

5

THE LIE

"Didn't you hear me, Max? You've been offered a place at Castle Toward music retreat against thousands of other applicants. This is as good as it gets. At least try and show some excitement." Barbara Beaton, Head of Music, stared at him, perplexed at his reaction.

Max stood awkwardly, forcing an unconvincing smile. He felt embarrassed. He knew the household budget would never stretch to an expensive luxury such as the retreat. It was already a struggle with his mother working two jobs, and the last thing she needed was another bill that wasn't a necessity.

"What's up, Max, aren't you happy?" his teacher persisted.

"Yes Miss, it's just that I won't be able to make it."

"You can't be serious, Max. You have to. Try to understand how important this is. It's life changing."

"I know, Miss, but it's my aunt. I'll be visiting her in Cornwall at the time of the retreat." Max pushed his long fringe out of his eyes and waited for the repercussion.

Miss Beaton's face was a picture of disappointment. "I have no doubt you'll have plenty of time in your life to visit your aunt, countless times. Opportunities like this only come once. You have to make whatever sacrifices you can to be there. Some of the greatest violinists are giving their time to you and the others. One-to-one coaching! It's the stuff of dreams, Max. You have to be there."

"Miss, I would love to go, but my aunt is seriously ill." Max felt dreadful telling a deliberate lie. He knew Miss Beaton had worked hard to get him this placement.

"I'll talk to your mother, and explain how important this is for your future."

"No, Miss, please don't. She's stressed enough with her sister dying."

Miss Beaton was surprised at his outburst; he was usually so quiet. She hadn't realised things were so strained for him. "Okay, Max, it's your choice, but it's one I'm sure you'll regret. Please wait there a moment." She sat at her desk and wrote frantically for a few minutes. Signing off with a flourish, she folded the paper in three and placed it in an envelope addressed to Mrs Bruford. "Please give this letter to your mother. It's not about the retreat, so don't worry. It's a letter explaining how well you're doing."

"Are you sure, Miss?"

"Perfectly."

"Can you promise me this letter doesn't mention the retreat?"

"I swear on everything important to me. This letter does not mention the music retreat." She crossed her heart; a sign he knew she wouldn't make if it were untrue.

Max toyed with the idea of opening the letter on his walk home from school through Wimbledon Common. He took it out and held it up to the light. He tried to peel back the flap, but it started to separate from the envelope. Opening the letter would put him in deeper trouble, so he placed it back in his bag.

Letting himself into his house, Max left the letter on the kitchen table and went to his room to practise his scales. Later his mother called him downstairs for dinner. He sat down to his favourite: sausage, egg and chips.

"How was your lesson today?"

"Good. Miss Beaton seems happy with me and the effort I'm putting in."

"So I see," she said, reading through the letter.

Max froze at the sight of it. "Did she say she was pleased?"

"She is positively glowing." She began to read out snippets. "'Max is enormously gifted when he plays violin.' And on the next line, 'No other student comes close to his level of performance.' She finishes with, 'His playing is exceptional.'"

Max breathed out slowly, thankful Miss Beaton hadn't mentioned their discussion that morning. He speared a sausage with his fork and dipped it into his egg, the yolk running down towards his fork.

"There's one thing Miss Beaton mentions that I don't understand. Hopefully you can help me?"

Max's mouth went dry, and he couldn't swallow the piece of sausage in his mouth. He was sure Miss Beaton was going to mention the retreat.

"Miss Beaton writes: 'I'm saddened to hear of your sister's illness. Max is clearly troubled by this. I hope your journey to see her in Cornwall next May goes well and she recovers fully if, of course, that's possible.'"

Max sat with his head down. He pulled the dry piece of sausage from his mouth and put it on his plate.

"Now, seeing as I don't have a sister, I'm trying hard to work out why Miss Beaton would think I did, especially after such praise. I'm assuming she has you mixed up with someone else in your class?" His mother put the letter down and stared at him.

Max remained silent.

"Well?"

Max continued to stare at his lap.

"I've never known you to lie to me, Max. However, right now, looking at your body language, I'm beginning to lose all trust in you. Explain to me what Miss Beaton is referring to."

He changed position and stared at his feet. He wanted to run away.

"If you don't tell me what's going on, I'll be at the school first thing tomorrow morning to ask your teacher myself. So your explanation better be a good one."

He couldn't look at her. He was furious at Miss Beaton. She said she wouldn't mention anything and now it was all coming out.

"Are you going to tell me what's happening, or will I deal with it at school tomorrow morning?"

Hot tears spilled down Max's cheeks, dripping onto his dinner plate beside his ruined dinner. He couldn't bear to think how much he had upset his mother. Unable to meet her gaze, he looked down to see his knees shaking uncontrollably. Knowing something must be very wrong, she reached out to him but he pushed her away and ran upstairs to his room. He jammed a chair against the door and lay sobbing on top of the blankets.

Five minutes later he heard a knock on his bedroom door. He didn't answer.

"Max, you need to let me in. Whatever this is about we

can fix it, like we always do. I know you must have had a good reason to tell Miss Beaton what you did."

He got up and moved the chair away from the door, then sat on the edge of his bed. As his mother entered, he buried his head in his hands, frightened to look at her.

"I'm sorry, Mum, I didn't want you to know anything about this."

"Clearly you didn't, but obviously Miss Beaton did."

"She shouldn't have written to you."

"I'm not so sure about that, Max. She has the right to, especially if she thinks something is troubling you. Tell me the whole truth now and I won't visit her tomorrow. But, if you lie to me, even once, we will both be going to the Principal's office first thing in the morning. Is that clear?"

Max nodded. He wiped his eyes with a tissue and took a deep breath. He explained his conversation with Miss Beaton and how she insisted on him going to the retreat. He knew they couldn't afford it. He told her how he'd lied to avoid her getting a letter inviting him to the expensive ten-day visit to Scotland.

"Max, I know you did this to protect me, but you shouldn't have."

"Well, we can't afford it. You've said many times we have no money left at the end of each week."

"How much is the retreat?"

"Expensive, that's how much. I know the type of people who will go, I meet them at orchestra classes. They don't care about money and if I'm honest, I don't even want to be with them. Let's leave it there."

"I want you to go, Max. It doesn't matter what the other kids think about money. If Miss Beaton thinks this would help advance you to another level, we should at least look at it. Don't you think so? After everything we've been through to get you to this level?"

"I don't want to go. We can't afford it. You can't work any more hours, or we'll never see each other. Look how tired you are every night."

"Okay, I'll write a letter to Miss Beaton, thanking her for the invitation and tell her we'll consider it for next year."

"I'm okay with that. By then, I can also have a part-time job that should give us some extra money. What are you going to say about your dying sister, can't you say she passed away?"

"No, Max, we can't lie about something that serious. I'll be honest with her, and we'll need to live through the consequences, together."

"I'll be the laughing stock, Mum. Everyone will know I lied."

"I don't think Miss Beaton would say anything. But if it does come out, we'll face it like grown-ups."

"Just let it go, Mum, don't say anything."

"I have to deal with it, and I promise you it will be okay. These situations are never as bad as your mind thinks it will be. You did what you did for the right reasons. You didn't lie for personal gain; you were trying to protect me. Believe me, we've been through worse together."

She went downstairs. Max knew she wanted to send him to the retreat and if there were a way, she would make it happen. Since his dad left, she'd struggled to keep them in basic living standards. Each month they were barely scraping by. He knew the support money she received didn't even cover their rent.

He remembered when his dad left them and how distraught his mother was. His departure had come as a shock to her as they were a good match and had so much love for each other, every day seemed so perfect. Twelve amazing years they had spent together, or so his mum had thought.

It was such a silly thing that started the arguments and Max knew it was his fault. He still wasn't sure if his mother had forgiven him. He missed his dad, especially as he had stopped visiting. His only communication now via birthday cards containing cash. Max wanted to thank him, but they had no idea where he lived. He had disappeared.

The arguments started not long after Max was loaned a violin from school. Max loved it at once and told his parents he wanted to be a musician. But his father was having none of it and repeated several times there had never been any musicians in the family.

His mum could see he had talent and wanted to encourage him more, as he enjoyed it so much. His dad pushed Max towards sciences, but he had little interest in them, although he did try.

The bitter arguing became a nightly occurrence. As he practised each night, he could hear their voices raised, louder each time. He pleaded with them not to fight over his music and eventually gave up the violin. He decided he wouldn't be the cause of them fighting; he wanted things back the way they were. His dad's mood changed, and for a while things improved, the violin being now a thing of the past. But his mum couldn't live this way and stood her ground, adamant that her son should follow his dream of being a musician.

One day his mum came home to find an empty wardrobe and a note left on the bed. She never could fathom why their marriage collapsed. They had loved each other so intensely for so long, and she thought they were together for life. It was hard for Max to understand how they became so destructive over his choice of music: the very thing that brings love and harmony to most people.

His mother was a wreck at first, ashamed to tell her family and friends her husband had left her. For months when people called for him, she made excuses, saying he was working away or job hunting. Little by little she let people know, and their reactions were always one of surprise. They too thought they were the perfect couple.

In the midst of his upset, confusion and guilt, Max wondered why his mum had stuck to her principles and broken the family home. It was such a high price to pay. He knew he would not have chosen music if he had known in advance the irreversible rift it would cause. After a few months had passed, he asked his mum why she didn't just let it go.

"If you truly love something, Max, nothing should stand in your way," she replied. "This was all about your dream. It was the first thing you really believed in, and someone else was trying to take it away from you through ignorance and selfishness."

"But I lost my dad because of it."

"True. But what kind of man doesn't support his own son in whatever endeavour he wants to pursue? A real father would have encouraged you to follow your dreams, not to take your happiness away and force you into things you don't like. What kind of husband tells his wife he won't live with her if she doesn't back down? That's tyranny, and we won't live like that, however hard it is without him."

"I didn't know all these things, Mum."

"It's not your fault. If anyone is to blame, it's me and your father. We failed you. I wanted our family so much to be a place of harmony, a safe place. But you have to have principals and stick with them. If someone has a belief, it's up to those around them to support them through the hardest times, so they never quit. That's what you and I have done; we're supporting each other. For some reason, your father couldn't find it in himself to support you. I wish I knew why, but I'm still none the wiser."

That evening, she wrote a letter to Miss Beaton and put it in his school bag.

"Give this to Miss Beaton first thing in the morning," she said.

Max nodded. He wasn't happy, but knew he had to face the music.

The next morning he put the letter on Miss Beaton's desk and left the classroom before she arrived.

Miss Beaton read the letter once her class had settled down to their work.

Dear Miss Beaton,

Thank you for your kind words about Max's music study. He is doing well, and I too am proud of his progress.

Regarding your kind words about my sister: I have to be upfront with you and tell you that Max lied to you. I do not have a sister, and certainly not an ill one.

His reasons for lying were noble, but unfortunately, a lie is a lie. I will deal with him for this inexcusable behaviour. I am sorry he involved you in this affair, but I can tell you he was only trying to protect me.

As a single mother, raising Max has left us in a position as such that we have little to no spare money. With my pitiful earnings, we barely manage to survive each week, and certainly couldn't afford to pay for the musician's retreat.

That is the reason Max lied to you: to save me from the embarrassment of having no money.

We both appreciate your intentions in considering Max. Unfortunately, we have to decline your kind invitation. Perhaps if our situation improves next year, we can organise for him to go then.

Regards,

Mary Bruford

P.S. I would hope you could keep Max's indiscretion between us, as it is not for others to judge our financial situation. By all means, give him a punishment for lying to you.

Miss Beaton finished reading the letter. The most gifted pupil ever to pass through her classroom in thirty years and he couldn't afford the retreat. How was this possible? She screamed inside, wondering what the odds were of this happening.

She vowed that somehow she would send Max to the retreat, even if she had to pay for it herself.

6

THE HEADMASTER

The following week, Miss Beaton knocked hard on the solid oak door of the headmaster's office, and waited. After a few minutes and no activity, she popped her head through the small sliding window of the secretary's office. Ms MacLeod, the dedicated workhorse of the school admin, sat typing furiously.

"He's in," she shouted, her gaze remaining focused on the task in hand. "Just wait."

Miss Beaton straightened herself up, almost to attention. She brushed herself down, picking the odd piece of fluff from her suit. She studied the nameplate on the door: Mr Marcus – Headmaster. *Yes, but for how long?* she wondered.

As she walked in circles following the pattern of the black and white floor tiles, her eyes moved to the large oak Headmasters' Hall of Fame board hanging in the reception area, where she read through the long list of previous headmasters and their years of service. She wasn't impressed. *The ego of these people,* she thought. Mr Marcus was the tenth Headmaster of Mosley Grammar since she arrived.

That was thirty years ago when she first walked though these doors as a young and timid assistant music teacher. She wondered what the hell was wrong with these people. These headmasters never stayed for any sensible length of time to deliver continuity of leadership. She looked through the list, and apart from a couple of long termers, most of them only managed two to three years.

With her fist clenched she knocked louder than the first time. Ms MacLeod glared at her through the window. "Patience, Miss Beaton, he knows you are waiting."

"My appointment is at one-thirty, Ms MacLeod. It is now quarter to two. I find it rude and demeaning when one has a pre-arranged appointment, and the other person fails to show. I also have to be back in class shortly."

"Miss Beaton. Tell me which part of "he knows you are waiting" you do not understand."

"I find that equally offensive, Ms MacLeod, especially if he knows his pre-arranged appointment is standing at his door. It's bloody – "

Miss Beaton's rant ended mid-sentence as the headmaster's office door swung open.

"Ah, Ms..." The headmaster looked at Ms MacLeod.

"Miss Beaton, Head of Music," his secretary said.

"Of course, Miss Beaton, sorry to keep you waiting. You know what it's like, I had an appointment with a chicken sandwich and had to catch up with what's happening in the world." He gestured behind him to the newspaper that lay across his desk. "Anyway, you said you had something important to tell me. You're not leaving, are you?"

"No sir, I am not leaving, not until you carry me out in a box. This school is my life, sir."

"That's what I like to hear, dedication. It's hard to find it these days."

Miss Beaton had no time for the "dedication" speech, especially as it was the headmasters who kept leaving. She pushed on.

"I'm here to request the school finds some funds to send one of my pupils to a music retreat in Scotland."

"Eh, what? What do you mean by 'find some funds'? We are not a charity. We don't have any funds, Miss ... um ..."

"Beaton, sir," Ms MacLeod offered helpfully.

Miss Beaton glared at her, wishing the headmaster would do her the courtesy of inviting her into his office. "Mr Marcus, I think we better have funds or someone's in trouble. Last year our summer and Christmas concerts raised over four thousand pounds. You said you would re-invest this money into the music department and we haven't seen a penny since."

The headmaster looked at the music teacher now with contempt. She was too self-assured, making all these demands. "Listen, Beaton."

"Miss or Ms, sir."

"*Miss* Beaton." The headmaster didn't like being corrected, especially on how he addressed his staff or in front of his secretary. "We don't have funds for personal trips for a favourite pupil. If we did this for one pupil, we'd have every parent wanting us to fund their child. Sorry, but I'm afraid it's a straightforward no from me."

"You haven't heard my story yet. It's important, sir."

"And I would love to hear your story, but we've run out of time. Try the Parent Teacher Council. They like fuzzy, feel-good things like this."

"What do you mean, I've run out of time? You owe me fifteen minutes, and I demand you hear me out."

The noise from the typewriters in the background went

from clattering at a fair speed to a deadly silence as the secretaries behind the screen listened in.

"Demand? Owe you? I'm sorry, Miss Beaton, but your thinking isn't quite straight. I owe you nothing and don't you ever demand anything from me. You're forgetting your place and to whom you're speaking. I'm asking you to think carefully before you say something stupid. If you do, we'll be finding you a new job in some elementary school in the middle of nowhere." He leaned his face in close to hers, an old army trick he had learnt to intimidate the men. "Is that clear?" His bright red face was covered in droplets of sweat.

Miss Beaton tensed at the sheer volume coming directly at her, then composed herself. Although she felt intimidated, she wasn't going to let him see her crumble. She spoke calmly. "You've made me stand outside waiting when we had an appointment at one-thirty. This is the time we should've been discussing my request, but you were eating lunch and reading newspapers. I could demand my fifteen minutes, but I'm hoping your sensibilities take over and help you realise your mistake."

Ms MacLeod's face was a study.

"Demand *again*, Miss Beaton. No one makes any demands on me. I am the principal of this school; I'm in charge."

"If you are in charge, sir, then act like it. Listen to my story as I won't be leaving until you do." She pushed past him into his office and sat down on the leather couch opposite his desk.

The headmaster was enraged at her boldness. Who did she think she was, sitting on his couch with her arms folded? He'd never dealt with the music department before. He considered them the same as arts and drama and saw them all as 'holiday' subjects. Subjects you took when you couldn't keep up with real education, like English, physics and maths.

"Okay, Miss Beaton, you can have your fifteen minutes," he looked at his watch, "and not a second more. Be aware, however, that the answer will be no." He shut the door and took a seat behind his desk.

Miss Beaton ignored his last comment and proceeded with her story about Max and how gifted he was. She told him of the boy's domestic situation. She described his broken family and how his mother couldn't afford to send her son on what would be a significant moment in the boy's life: "To work with these top violinists."

Mr Marcus stared at his watch while she talked. "Time's up. I heard your story, very sad. I understand your dilemma. Can't you send him next year?"

"No sir, it has to be now. Now or never, it's that serious at this stage of his development."

"How much would it cost us?"

"A thousand pounds, covering the transport, the course and some spending money."

"And where are we going to get a thousand pounds from?"

"The school concert money of four thousand pounds was raised by musicians. We are trying to help probably the best musician ever to enter this school. This is the equivalent of sending a student to the Olympics Games, that's how serious it is. Give me one thousand pounds, sir, and you'll still have three thousand for other things."

"I couldn't possibly decide this off the cuff. You should know there are processes. It would take a few weeks. I'll need to ask the other teachers and school board members."

Miss Beaton produced a sheet of paper. Since Mary Bruford's letter a week ago, she had been planning this encounter. It was titled *Support for Max Bruford*. On it was the signature of nearly every teacher in the school. Even the department heads had signed the sheet. All except the Physical Education department, who had started to question using the funds for a trip they wanted for the cricket team, something the headmaster believed in.

"I have most of the teachers in this school supporting Max Bruford. The others weren't here or were off on leave, and so I couldn't get to them."

"You've certainly done your homework, Miss Beaton, most resourceful." Mr Marcus read through the list. Everyone who was someone at the school had signed it. "Either this boy must be very popular, or you are a very persuasive person."

"He is a popular boy, sir. Can I tell Max and his mother we are going to help him?"

"Does it have to be this quickly?"

"Yes, sir, it has to happen today. What if I tell the media the headmaster heard of Max's plight and spearheaded a campaign to find the funds? You would receive all the glory."

Mr Marcus was quiet as he thought it through.

"It would look good in the local paper and to all the teachers and the boy, sir."

"Well, I wouldn't want to take all the credit, but I suppose as a figurehead I am happy that you use my name and spread the word how I helped young..."

"Max, sir. The boy's name is Max."

"Of course, it is. I knew that. Okay, you have your funds. Bring the boy and his mother here to meet me and bring a reporter too – publicity for the school, of course."

"Alright, but I'll need a letter right now for Ms MacLeod, explaining the release of the funds."

"Right now, Beaton?"

"Yes sir, right now. And remember, it's Miss Beaton."

"Of course, it is. Old army habit, calling people by their second name."

"I understand, Marcus." She smiled.

The headmaster stiffened.

"It doesn't feel nice, sir, does it?"

Mr Marcus went to his desk and pulled out a blank letterhead. Quickly, he scribbled a letter to his secretary to release the funds and handed it to Miss Beaton.

"Thank you, sir; you don't know what you have done. Never forget this name: Max Bruford. You will be instrumental in his success, excuse the pun."

"Pun, Miss Beaton, what pun?"

"It doesn't matter, sir."

"I like you, Beaton. You are deputy head material."

This time she ignored his mistake on her name. "I've been offered the position three times, sir; it's not for me. I'm a musician, and I'm here to inspire young musicians. Not to lose my life bogged down in admin and school boards and petty squabbles. But thank you for the recognition."

With that, she stalked out of the headmaster's office and handed the letter to Ms MacLeod.

"I can't approve this, how did you – "

"Just organise the money for me please, Ms MacLeod. It's not your place to question it. I will pick it up tomorrow, cash."

Miss Beaton made her way back to class feeling satisfied with the outcome.

7

GOOD NEWS

Mary Bruford was preparing a packed lunch for Max when a knock on her front door startled her. She froze for a few seconds. Max was upstairs playing the violin, and no one ever visited them in the evening. She hoped her landlord wasn't going to ask them to leave as he had threatened.

She peered through the spy hole on the front door but could only see a dark shape. The outside light was broken, making it hard to see who was there.

She put the security chain on without making a sound and opened the door slightly. A woman with a long coat and hat stood there.

"Can I help you?"

"Mrs Bruford? It's Barbara Beaton, Max's music teacher.

"Oh, sorry, I wasn't expecting you. Is it about the letter?"

"In a way, yes. Would it be possible to discuss the matter inside? It feels awkward standing outside in the dark." Miss Beaton had had her fill of waiting in people's doorways.

"Of course, so sorry, come in. You'll have to excuse the mess; I wasn't expecting visitors."

"No need to apologise. You should see the state of my place."

Miss Beaton came into the room as her host went to the kitchen area to put the kettle on. "Are these your drawings?" she asked, admiring the collection on the table

"Oh, it's a hobby of mine, I draw teddy bears in charcoal and sell them to the local shops."

"They're very good. I'm sure whoever sees or buys one of these gets a permanent smile."

"Yes, I seem to get a good reaction from them. Although shopkeepers always want them for nothing and then price them high."

Miss Beaton flicked through the pile of drawings until tea was served.

"Mrs Bruford, we need to discuss Max."

"Call me Mary, it's less formal. Is he behaving himself?"

"Yes, of course, he's a wonderful pupil. A credit to you, Mary."

"Is it about the letter I sent you?"

"Indirectly, yes. It's more to do with the musicians' retreat."

"I thought I had made myself clear we can't afford for Max to go, not this year anyway. It's hundreds of pounds we don't have."

"Not to worry. I am the bringer of good news. Can you call Max down so we can discuss it?"

Mary handed Miss Beaton her cup of tea. She didn't have any biscuits and thought it best not to mention the fact. She grabbed the bannister at the bottom of the stairs and called Max.

The distant sound of a violin playing ended abruptly. Footsteps came hurrying downstairs.

"What's happening?" Max stopped dead when he saw his teacher looking at him. "Miss Beaton, he looked over to his mother, I'm in trouble aren't I? Am I being expelled?"

His mind was racing, his gaze passing back and forth between the two women. He couldn't make any sense of why Miss Beaton might have come to his home.

"Max, come and sit down. I have something I want to discuss with you," said Miss Beaton.

"I'm getting kicked out for lying, aren't I?"

"Of course not. Let me explain why I'm here." Miss Beaton looked around the room. It was scant in its furnishings, which she was sure wasn't through choice. "I'm here to discuss the retreat in Scotland."

"There's nothing to discuss, Miss. I shouldn't have made up that story about my aunt – "

Miss Beaton raised her hand to stop him talking. "It's good news. I asked the headmaster if he was willing to apportion some school funds to fund your trip." She smiled. "When he heard it was you, Max, he couldn't give me the money quickly enough. He already knew of your talents and said if the school can't support Max Bruford then who can it support? He immediately wrote a letter releasing the funds." With that, she reached into her pocket, pulled out an envelope and placed it on the table.

"What's this?" asked Mary.

"A thousand pounds."

"No!" She stared at the music teacher. "It can't be!"

Miss Beaton's smile grew wider. "It is. I promise it's all yours."

"But that amount of money is far too much. The retreat doesn't cost that much, does it? There must be at least four hundred pounds above the fees."

"I know, but don't concern yourself with that. Tomorrow you have to book Max on the course and pay for it immediately. They won't keep his place any longer; it's that critical."

"I will, I promise. I can't thank you enough. But what about the rest of the money?"

"Buy Max some new clothes and toiletries and give him some spending money."

"But that will still leave a few hundred left."

"That's correct. I told the headmaster Max only had a cheap practice violin and if he is to play with the best in the world, he will need a new one. That's why we got the extra money."

"But ... he already has a good violin." Mary's brow furrowed. "It's of reasonable quality."

"I know. Indeed, it's better than most student violins. Let's just say the school contributed towards it."

As the extent of Miss Beaton's generosity dawned, Mary began to shake her head. "No, we can't accept this money; I honestly feel quite shocked."

"I'm afraid you'll have to accept it or you'll get me into trouble." The music teacher was smiling but it was clear she wasn't going to take no for an answer. "The school owes my pupils rewards like this. The music department has raised more money than any other department and we never get anything in return. Consider this donation to Max our first real investment." Finishing her tea, she got up to leave. "I'm feeling good," she announced. "What about you two?"

Max stepped forward. "I don't know what to say, Miss,

thank you. You've helped me so much. I'll never be able to repay you for your generosity."

"Max, I want you to go to the retreat and absorb everything you can from the master violinists. Then come back and prove to the world that you are the genius I believe you to be. If you can do this, you will prove I was right to have so much faith in you. Make me proud. That will be my payback."

Tears shone in Max's eyes. "I will, Miss. I'll do my best."

Miss Beaton shook both their hands. She paused at the door. "Oh, one more thing. It would be helpful when you accept this award that you praise the headmaster. Tell the local paper how much you appreciate him supporting you on the retreat. If you can do that, it will make life easier for me next time I try to help another pupil."

Max nodded.

"Before you go, could you please wait just one moment?" Mary excused herself to the kitchen, then returned and handed Miss Beaton a large square parcel wrapped in brown paper and tied up with string.

"What's this?"

"A small gift. It should make you smile, or you could give it to a friend or child if you prefer."

Miss Beaton's eyes widened. "I'll pay you for it."

"I think you've paid us more than enough."

The teacher smiled, placed the parcel under her arm and walked out the door. Max and his mum waved to her from the window. They saw her put on her hat before disappearing into the darkness beyond the street lamps.

8

FIRST JOURNEY

The coach park was desolate and cold at six-thirty in the morning, making Max feel anxious as he waited with his mother for the coach to arrive. He was looking forward to being at the retreat and was sure it would be music heaven. But his mum's face was paler than normal and Max was worried about leaving her on her own. This would be the first time they had been separated since his father had left them.

Max was looking forward to visiting another country for the first time. Luckily for him, it was Scotland and not somewhere on the other side of the world. He had never been away before and tried to stop trembling, blaming it on the cold. He couldn't let his mum know he was afraid or she would get nervous too.

A car drove in, and Max wondered who would visit an empty coach park this early in the morning. It stopped beside them, and Miss Beaton got out.

"Miss! Why are you here?"

"I came to see you off, Max, to make sure you got on the coach."

"Oh, don't worry. I can't wait to go."

Miss Beaton smiled. "You'll love it, Max. You'll be working with the best there is. I didn't tell you before, but I was offered a place like this over thirty years ago, and I couldn't go for similar reasons to your own. I've regretted it all my life. That's why I place so much hope in you."

"I appreciate you helping me get here. I'm sorry it didn't happen for you, Miss. It makes a huge difference if you have someone believing in you and fighting your corner."

"Not to worry, it's a long time past now. Things worked out differently for me but I wouldn't change helping students for any other job. One day I'll be proven right about you."

"I hope so."

The coach pulled into the coach park. It was already half full with kids, their noses pressed up against the windows, curious to see who would be next to get on.

Max looked at his mum, who had started to well up. Miss Beaton took her arm and led them both to the back of the coach. "If you want to hug Max, do it here where the other kids can't see you. They will see it as a sign of weakness."

Mary nodded and turned to her son. "Look at you, all grown up. A young man now and almost as tall as your father."

Max was surprised at the comment as his mother rarely mentioned him.

"Promise me you'll think of me every day."

"I promise. It's only ten days. I'll be back before you know it."

"I know, but I'm going to miss you. If you're allowed to use a phone, try and call me, day or night, it doesn't matter what time it is."

"I will, Mum."

He picked up his bag to go on the coach, but she pulled him close to her and hugged him. "Please don't forget to let me know you are okay. I'll need that call, just to hear your voice."

Max smiled. "I won't forget. I'll call as soon as I get the chance."

Miss Beaton took Max by the arm and led him to the coach stairs, where she shook his hand. "Okay, Max, show them who has the best music teacher in the country."

Max nodded in relief, then climbed aboard. For a moment he had thought Miss Beaton was going to hug him. He walked down the rows until he found an empty seat. His mum and Miss Beaton stood at the side as the driver put the coach into gear, then began to drive off. His mum waved and he raised his hand slightly to let her know he had seen her. He could see she was trying to be brave, smiling while wiping her hands under her eyes.

As they moved onto the open road, Max felt alone even in the midst of a coach full of kids. A couple of boys introduced themselves and asked Max if he had any sweets. He took a packet out of his pockets, and the boys snatched it and disappeared, laughing. Max felt stupid and wanted to go home.

They stopped a number of times on the way to Scotland to pick up other students carrying instruments of all shapes and sizes. At Carlisle, a girl came on and due to the lack of any other seats, sat beside Max.

"Is it okay to sit here?"

"Sure," said Max. "I think it's the only seat left."

"My name is Lily. Short for Lily-Anne, but no one ever calls me that."

"Hi, I'm Max, short for something I don't ever want to

remember."

Lily smiled. "Go on, tell me."

"No, definitely not." Max looked out the window. The hills were getting bigger. He was surprised that with so much countryside, there were so few buildings. Only cottages dotted the landscape. Scotland certainly looked different to London.

"What instrument do you play?" she asked.

"Violin."

"You any good?"

"Not particularly. My teacher thinks I've got 'something special' in my playing style."

"Mine too. I play the cello as my first instrument and piano as my second."

"Awesome. Bagpipes are my second instrument."

"Really? You play the bagpipes?"

Max grinned and shook his head.

Lily punched him his arm. "I almost believed you."

"Almost! I think for a moment there you had visions of me in a kilt, screeching and wailing."

They both laughed and chatted for the rest of the journey.

The coach eventually stopped at a large car park on the edge of a river. The driver shouted back to the children, "We're getting on a ferry for half an hour. You can all get off to stretch your legs and get some fresh air."

On the ferry, Max and his newfound friend stayed together. They stood at the front of the boat and watched the swell of the water. It was Max's first time on a boat, and he wasn't keen on the motion. Lily stood perfectly balanced.

"You have to go with the rhythm, Max. Watch the swell of the waves and balance yourself, so you rise and fall with them. You'll feel much better."

Max stood in the same position as her, legs apart and knees slightly bent. The boat was rising and falling, and as it did so, Max shifted his weight to counteract it. She was right; this felt good. He stared into the water as the foam ran along the top of the swells, marvelling at the changing patterns and wave sizes. He was fascinated by the way the sunlight caught the water, making it dance and sparkle as the waves went through their cycle.

Halfway across, the water became far more turbulent. Waves came crashing over the front of the ramp at the front. Lily ran back towards the coach, but Max stayed where he was, mesmerised. Some of the water hit him; it was freezing cold, but refreshing, leaving a taste of salt in his mouth. He watched wave after wave, dark grey and black, white foam breaking. Max had never been on a river like this before. There was something primitive about how he felt at this moment: exposed to the elements and witnessing the true power of nature.

He stared into the water; the swelling waves wielding their hypnotic effect, until Max heard something he never thought possible: music. It sounded as if it was coming from the river, in sync with the rhythm of the waves, coming towards him. He shook his head, trying to make sense of it. The melody was delicate and haunting, almost as if the river was calling to him. Max's head was filled with the most beautiful sounds and music he had ever heard. It was as if he was witnessing nature first hand, as if the soul of the sea was talking to him in its language. He needed to remember this and write the music down.

Lily came running across the deck to fetch him.

"Max, are you okay? You need to get back on the coach; you're soaked through."

"Can you hear music, Lily?"

"What are you talking about? There's only the sound of the wind and the waves ... unless you can hear the coach radio?"

Max looked across the surface of the river towards the shore. He could hear a symphony rising from the depths, or was it coming from within himself?

"C'mon, get back on the coach." Lily grabbed his arm and pulled him away from the handrail. He was grinning from ear to ear. The others laughed at the state of him; his shirt and hair were soaked through. The ferry arrived, and the men on the dock caught the ropes and anchored the boat to the pier. The coach drove off the ferry and headed along the coast road towards Castle Toward.

After half an hour, the coach announced its arrival at the retreat by bumping up the driveway. The kids were jostled roughly as the wheels hit pothole after pothole. The poorly managed entrance wasn't the best first impression. Castle Toward looked dark and grey with ivy covering most of the front of the building.

"Stay close by," said Lily. "You can be my friend."

Max smiled. He liked her and was glad she'd sat next to him. It was good to have someone to talk to, especially here, so far away from home. Most of the other kids had been boastful about how good they were as musicians, but Lily wasn't showy like them. "You can be my friend too," he replied.

They reached above to get their hand luggage and moved down the aisle towards the door. Lily put her hands on his shoulders as if they were elephants on parade. He hadn't felt a girl touch him like this before and it sent shivers down his spine.

"Are you okay?" asked Lily.

Max nodded. "Fine." His voice came out in a rasp.

9

CASTLE TOWARD

"Please leave your bags in the hallway and go through to the dining room," a man shouted above the noise of the assembled crowd as each student carried their cases into the central area of the building. "The helpers in blue jumpers will show you where to go."

Once inside, Max was amazed at how grand everything was. The broad staircase made from dark wood curved upwards towards the next floor. The posts at the bottom of the stairs had lion's heads carved on them. Chandeliers sparkled from the hundreds of tiny lights shining through the crystal droplets. Paintings adorned the walls: animals, hunts and Scottish landscapes, moody and overpowering. Max was sure these were the most significant paintings he'd ever seen.

The helpers in blue jumpers led the newly arrived travellers through to the dining room. Six adults were talking at what Max gathered to be the head table. He was sure he recognised one of the men, although he couldn't think why, as he didn't know anyone in Scotland.

A woman who looked as if she was in charge clapped

her hands. "Silence, please." Dressed head to toe in black, she was slim and probably about fifty years old. Her features were sharp. "I am Ms Falconer, and I will be in charge of your stay. If you have any issues, you come to me. No doubt you want to find where you are sleeping and go to the bathrooms after such a long journey. Upstairs there are four dormitories. Look at the list outside each room to find your name and where you will be sleeping. The bathrooms are next to the dormitories. When I finish speaking you can go upstairs and get a quick freshen up. Change into something more comfortable then come back down here in one hour precisely if you want to eat. Go!"

She clapped her hands together. The room cleared as everyone scrambled upstairs, laying their claim to whichever bed they thought best. There was a scuffle with two boys fighting over a bigger bed. Max went to the last bed in a row of three and placed his bag on top. He pushed his violin underneath. After washing and changing, he headed downstairs.

Most of the students were already sitting at the long dining tables when Max took his place. Staff members filled the tables with trays of hot food. Everyone filled their plates and ate for the next hour. There was a lot of chatter and some silences as the hungry mouths ate their fill. Seeing the students were bleary-eyed, Ms Falconer rapped the table to get everyone's attention.

"Today has been an exhausting day for you. After dinner I want everyone washed and into bed. Tomorrow morning after breakfast, we will explain the programme we have lined up. There will be an exciting study for you to excel as a soloist or as an orchestra member. Make sure you take time to enjoy this experience. It won't be all work and no play. There will be plenty of leisure time for walks to the beach and to build campfires. Some nights we will have live music under the stars, weather permitting, of course."

The students clapped and cheered.

Ms Falconer lifted her arms and pointed to the people beside her. "Our guests beside me are the musicians who have given up their valuable time. They work with the best orchestras in the world and so you are in for a treat. In the coming days, you will each get to work individually with these musicians. It's your duty to yourselves to learn from them and put the time and effort in like you've never done before. Listen carefully to our professionals. They will help you as much as they can. Some of their teachings may go against what you have been taught from your tutor back home, but that's okay."

Ms Falconer could see there wasn't much of a response coming from the exhausted students. She realised it would be better to wait until morning.

"Alright then! Off to bed with you, and no complaining."

10

AVERAGE AMONGST PEERS

Next morning Max had breakfast with Lily, before heading to the big hall together. Once again, Ms Falconer was there to take control. She raised her arms and lowered them slowly; the noise in the hall died down simultaneously. She addressed the students in a more formal tone than the night before.

"You are about to embark on a journey. Each one of you is here because you are special in your abilities. Back home you will be recognised as the top musicians in your schools. They will call you outstanding, prodigies, and many other titles. I'm sure you've all heard some of these terms.

"It's different here. At Castle Toward you are all gifted and you will soon realise everyone in this hall is as good or maybe even better than you. Being average amongst your peers is not something you will have experienced before. You may even be on the bottom rung here. If so, I want to say to you: Welcome to the real world."

There were some groans from the assembled students.

"Our industry consists of thousands of talented musicians all fighting for the same jobs. It can be a cut-throat business to get to the top positions with the best orchestras, so you have to raise your game. There are thousands of musicians out there who were once just like you. They too were labelled as being unique. Many of them are now working in orchestras, recording studios, teaching or giving private lessons.

"One day you will be them. Excellent musicians, trying to earn your way through life with your passion. You will play the best theatres and concert halls. You will work with some of the biggest names in all genres of music where the work of classically trained musicians is valued. It's your job to be out there, proving yourself.

"Your position is to take what you can from the next ten days. Ask yourself, do you want this lifestyle?"

Lily squeezed Max's arm. "This is exciting," she whispered.

Max didn't hear what she said; he was overwhelmed by her breath in his ear. It was similar to when she held on to his shoulders on the coach. As another unfamiliar tingle ran down his spine, he tried to focus back in on what Ms Falconer was saying.

"...what we are looking for amongst you are musicians that want to go beyond being an excellent player. We are looking for the virtuosos who won't settle for being first or second violinist. We want to find those amongst you who live and breathe playing your instrument, the ones interested in getting to the top. Who wants to be the virtuosos of your generation? Is there anybody here who wants that?"

A selection of hands shot up into the air. They had no doubt what they were aiming for.

Ms Falconer gestured to the musicians at her table. "I am sure you will know, or will have heard of my guests with us today. Every one of them has been where you are now, and yet all of them have hit the lofty heights that most musicians can only dream of.

"It's payback time for them. They remember the help others gave them. The support of their families and music teachers, the endless hours and patience, guiding them to become something valuable in the music world.

"One day, hopefully, you will return and payback to help other students. It doesn't matter where or when that happens, just remember it will be your chance to change another person's life."

Ms Falconer introduced the teachers by name. Max had heard of two of them. They must have been well known according to the oohs and aahs from the others. Max was assigned to the violinist, Mr Edward Parks. His recordings were in Miss Beaton's record collection, and Max had listened to them many times.

After the talk, they were all given a timetable to follow strictly for the next nine days. Max was assigned to a range of classes: one-to-one tuition, string masterclasses and orchestra practice. *This is going to be fun*, he thought.

He looked for Lily and was glad to see they shared a few classes together. Feeling not a little apprehensive, he headed promptly to his first one-to-one lesson with Mr Parks.

11

FIRST LESSON

As Ms Falconer had stated, Mr Parks, like the other guests, had played around the world many times. He'd had seven albums released in his name and had played on hundreds of different tracks for various composers. One of his career highlights was recording at Abbey Road Studios with one of the top symphony orchestras.

He regarded Max and his violin as he brought it from his case. "Can I see your instrument, please?"

Max handed it over. Mr Parks looked it up and down, then picked up his bow and drew it across the strings. He shone a torch into the F-holes and examined the label within.

"Where did you get this instrument?"

"My mother bought it from a second-hand music shop in London."

"She did well, very well. Do you know how much she paid for it?"

"I believe it was about two hundred pounds."

Mr Parks sprang out of his seat, picked up the instrument and played. Max hadn't heard the range of tones that now flowed from his violin. Why did it sound so different, warmer, more in-depth? It was like a new instrument. Max asked his mentor.

"Not a different instrument Max, a different player. A bad player can make a Stradivarius sound dreadful, and the best players can make an average instrument sound great. The instrument and the player have to work together. When you can do that, your violin will sound the way it does with me."

"You said my mum did well, sir. Is it a good instrument?"

"She got a bargain, Max. I would have paid between seven hundred and a thousand pounds for it. Look after it; it will get better with age and with you. Now let me hear you play."

Max started to play some Grade Eight pieces he had learnt. Mr Parks didn't look at him. He sat with his chair facing the open window, looking into the gardens. Max had heard Mr Parks wouldn't watch any pupils he worked with on their first lesson. He found it insulting but continued playing.

Mr Parks slammed his hand on the table beside him, making such a noise it startled Max. "Don't play that rubbish! It's nonsense, Max; it's dead men's music. Play something of your own. Play whatever it is you do to warm up or perhaps some tune you have written and play to yourself. Anything original. I don't need to hear another bad copy of someone else's music."

Max took fright. He hadn't been shouted at before by a teacher, especially in the first few minutes.

"Max, let me hear how you connect with your instrument and what you are capable of, not some supposed classic. They are only good for learning formats and structure for practice. You can never connect to that music. Only the composer knows what they wrote and what it meant to them. I want to hear Max Bruford and his music. If you haven't written anything, then play what you do when you practice and go off-piste when your mind wanders. The moments you are taken in by your instrument, where you express yourself."

Max felt sick. He knew what Mr Parks meant by playing off-piste, but it wasn't something he could force. He didn't know what to play; he had never played anything of his own.

Mr Parks reprimanded him again. "Son, you only have ninety minutes with me each day. Make every second count for us both. Don't freeze on me, and don't waste my time. How will you ever stand on a stage in the spotlight if you can't even play here where you have the luxury to make mistakes? You are never forgiven if you mess up in concert."

Max picked up his violin and tried to think what to play. He started to play up and down some scales. This wasn't what Mr Parks was looking for, but he kept playing, swapping rhythm and melody, trying to find something. He could see the back of Mr Parks's head shake; this wasn't going well. He was at a loss and ready to give up when the scene from the ferry came to mind. He heard the tune from the river in his head and started to play along to it. Max could see the water rise and fall and followed it with his bow. He watched the back of Mr Parks's head as he played. It began to sway and follow the music. He was sure his mentor was enjoying his tune.

Max built upon the melody, increasing the power of each stroke. As he raised his game, his intricate finger work allowed him to fall into the peaks and troughs of the waves, riding along them like the foam. He saw himself trying to balance on the boat as he counteracted his weight against their force. He fought the counter-balance with his bow, trying to stay true to his feelings. He could see the notes in his head and he followed them.

Edward Parks did something he had never done before on the first appraisal of a new student: he spun round in his chair to watch the young violinist.

Although difficult, Max managed to ignore him. He followed the tune he could now see clearly in his head. He had experienced this before but hadn't written the tune down or followed through with it. Now he realised he could see and play it live as he experienced it. He brought the tempo down until it settled into a lilt, soft and gentle, back and forth, barely moving. In his head, Max was watching the water lapping against the shore of the shale beach, the current dragging the stones back and forth.

Max was as lost in his music as he had ever been. He played without knowing where he was going next. What he played came rushing through him from a place he didn't know. The water seemed to be drawing him in further, he felt surrounded, going deeper and deeper, into an understanding of his music he never knew he had.

He could taste the sea, just like on the ferry and, as he came back towards his conscious level, he could feel moisture. With a jolt, he realised it was sweat running down his face onto his lips; his shirt was soaking. Max played the final notes and let the silence in the room take over. Finally, he dropped his violin and bow to his sides and bowed to the teacher.

"Is that what you wanted, sir?"

Edward Parks looked at Max, taken aback by what he had witnessed. This performance was like an old soul in a young body. This was way beyond his expectation of what he would find at the retreat.

"Who is the composer, Max? I don't know this piece."

"It's no one's, sir. I made it up as I played, just like you told me to."

"That tune was never made up in a day. There was too much depth to that music; you must have heard it before."

"No, sir. Honestly, I started not knowing where I was going and it just flowed through me."

"Perhaps you heard it somewhere, maybe from your music teacher's collection?"

"It is mine, sir. I created it as I played. Didn't you like it?"

"I did like it, very much. What's it called?"

"It doesn't have a name; that was my first time playing it. It was in my head."

"It reminded me of the ocean. I felt as if I was travelling on the sea."

"We were, sir; I was there too. That's where I got the song from on the ferry yesterday. That was my first time on a boat."

"Max, you need to write the music down. Do you think you can remember how to play this again?"

Max picked up his violin and played his tune. Mr Parks smiled, not something he did often. His first day, his first pupil and there was something very special about this boy. He wanted to play Max's tune.

"You have to give it a name, Max."

"Soul of the Sea."

"Yes, I like that. We'll explore this further tomorrow; for now, try to notate the music if you can. I may want you to play this in front of the other teachers, later on."

Max nodded. “Do you think I could make a career playing the violin, sir?”

“Yes, Max, everyone at the retreat can make a career playing music. I think the question is whether you can attain virtuoso status. It’s early days in this programme for you, however, by the end of the week we’ll have a more rounded view of your skills.”

“Thank you for the lesson. I listen to your records with my music teacher.”

“Excellent, maybe one day I’ll be listening to yours.” He smiled. “Same time tomorrow, Max.”

12

LILY

When Max wasn't in class or rehearsals, he would meet up with Lily. Together, they explored Castle Toward and the surrounding area. Before dinner each evening they headed to the beach to skim stones. Groups of seals lay on the rocks and Max wanted to adopt every one of them. His excitement got the better of him when a seal's head popped out the water close to shore.

The beach was also busy with birds poking their beaks into the sand, hunting for worms and crabs. A variety of gulls would pick up the larger shellfish and drop them onto the rocks. The shells would split open, revealing their gooey insides. A large heron stood like a silent statue at the water's edge, taking off when disturbed.

Max had never seen wildlife like this before, and marvelled at how close they could get to it. He could feel music stirring within him as he adapted to his new surroundings. But there was something else.

From behind his fringe, Max watched Lily's every movement, her hair straggly and blowing freely in the wind.

A slight redness appeared on her cheeks when she smiled. And she was so tactile – Max had never met anyone who touched him so much. He had been brought up never to touch anyone and to respect other people's space. Yet here he was with Lily holding his arm, rubbing his back or putting her hand on his knee. It was unnerving and yet felt so good at the same time.

As they scrambled across the rocks, she held his arm again. "Look at the seals; those look like seal pups." She leant on his shoulder while watching the wildlife. Max wasn't complaining. He just didn't know how to handle it.

The main challenge he faced was the music that flowed into his head when he was with her. When she smiled, he could hear bows dancing across violin strings. When she looked at him with that playful spark in her eyes, the music would draw him in further, closer to oblivion. What was happening to him?

Even as he watched the seals, he was beginning to hear his music, the notes floating in front of him. He could feel different instruments for different things. The sandpipers on the beach were always piccolos, while the seals were cellos and low notes from the trombones. The heron in all its grace was always a wall of strings playing to a beat and movement to match its wings.

"Have you heard about the lighthouse, Max?" Lily's voice startled him out of his daydream.

"I've heard a few things about it, yes. I saw it on the way here. It looks pretty cool."

"I could make us a picnic, and we could walk around it tomorrow if you want?"

"Not sure I want to go that close, Lily. Haven't you heard about the lighthouse keeper and how strange he and his wife are?"

"I did hear a rumour. It won't be true."

"Some of the boys reckon they're both over one hundred and fifty years old."

"That's just nonsense. I'm not sure that is even possible. People make things up."

"You're so right. Take my tutor, Mr Parks. People say how strange he is and yet I get on fine with him."

"He is strange, Max, very strange. Who doesn't look at their pupils when they are playing?"

"I thought about that. I think it's because he wants to hear them first. He doesn't want to be distracted by looks, shirt tails or gravy down the front of our jumpers."

"Never thought of that. Maybe you're right."

"Anyway, the lighthouse?"

"Well, I'd like to see it, but I'd rather not be freaked out by strange people who might lock us up, and then we would be stuck here forever."

Max smiled. He loved the faces Lily pulled and thought she had the strangest way of thinking. "That wouldn't be a bad thing. Would it?"

She grabbed his arm. "Let's go back to the castle. We need to get ready for dinner. I hope there's a pudding tonight."

"Me too. That steam pudding and custard was the best ever last night."

She nodded in agreement and gave Max's arm a squeeze.

He watched as she walked in front of him, admiring her tight blue jeans and cheesecloth shirt, which he could see through partly.

They didn't say much. Lily broke the silence.

"One of the boys in your dorm, Eliot from Cambridge, do you know him?"

"Yes, not too well, but he's okay."

"That's good. He asked me to be his girlfriend and also to partner with him for the Scottish country dancing on Friday night. Apparently, they're bringing in some local dancers to celebrate our week and teach us how to do a few reels and jigs."

Max stopped walking. The noise in his head sounded like an orchestra crashing into a wall. He couldn't speak.

"I know you don't like dancing. I'm the same, but I might give it a go, it could be fun."

Rage built up inside Max as he tried to prevent himself from screaming.

"Anyway, I told him thanks but no thanks as I already have a partner to dance with."

Max struggled to find the words. "You ... you have a partner? Who else has asked you?"

"Max, you are such a dumpling at times. Even when I take your arm, you don't take the hint. *You're* my partner." Lily wrapped her arms around Max and hugged him. He could smell her perfume and felt her hair brush against his face; a symphony was building in his head.

Lily smoothed her fingers through Max's fringe. "I wish my hair was like yours. It's so soft. I love touching it."

Max smiled. He loved it when Lily did this. He could feel her fingers brushing back and forth against his face. It gave him goosebumps.

"Oh, I almost forgot to say, it's a 'girls only' meeting tonight."

"Why girls only? What's happening?"

"We are getting a safety talk about women working in touring orchestras. The dangers of travelling with strange men, especially violinists like you." She grinned. "We are also learning how women should act when visiting different cultures."

"Sounds like a barrel of fun. I wonder why we're not getting the same talk."

"Because you are the men, the source of most of the problems." She smiled and punched him on the arm.

"I honestly can't wait until tomorrow to see you again. Can't we meet tonight? Even if it is only for five minutes?"

"No, Max! Meet me for breakfast tomorrow morning." She leaned forward to kiss him on the cheek and ran up the stairs.

Max stood still, trying to take it in. He was reeling from the kiss.

"Max, phone call for you."

Did Lily just ask me to be her boyfriend?

The boy shouted again. "Max, what's up with you? Your mum's on the phone. Third time today she's called. Where do you wander off to? You're never here."

Max ran to the house and grabbed the phone, his head swimming with thoughts of Lily. He was floating on air.

After apologising for at least ten minutes, he told his mum all the things that had been happening: the music, the wildlife and the beach.

"I've missed you so much, Max."

"Me too, Mum, I can't wait to come home and see you." He knew that was the right thing to say; he could hear her sigh out loud.

"As soon as you come home, we are heading out for a meal and to the pictures."

"As long as I can choose the film."

He thought it best not to mention Lily. His mum knew he was enjoying the retreat and was happy for him, that's all that mattered. They said their goodbyes and Max ran up to his room to lie on his bed and think about his day.

He recovered every memory of Lily he could. All the things she did, every gesture she made, the way her body moved – it was all music to him. The way she touched his arm. How her fingertips brushed his as she passed him a cup of milk at breakfast. Her knee nudging his under the table, her fingers running through his hair, the smell of her perfume sending him into freefall...

The pictures stuck in his head most, however, were her smile and the glint in her eyes. They knocked him for six. Max could see the music forming in his head again, different from the last time. He grabbed his violin, a pencil and some paper, and started to write down the music he was seeing as he thought of her. After two hours, he had most of his tune annotated. He wrote one word at the top of the page.

Lily.

13

THE TEASE

Max and Lily laughed and giggled over breakfast, much to the annoyance of those around them. At one point, Lily leaned over and traced love hearts with her finger onto his palm under the table.

"Let's go for a walk this morning," she said. "We could climb a hill and get a view of the boats on the river."

Max was tempted. But he had his full assessment from his tutor and the other teachers at ten o'clock.

"I'd rather be with you, Lily, but I can't miss my assessment. My mum would be horrified if I didn't turn up for this."

Lily stood up and led Max outside. "Of course. I forgot you were on this morning. You're streets ahead of everyone so you have nothing to worry about. I want to hear what they have to say about you. What pieces are you playing for them?"

"I'm playing the tune I wrote the other day, which I've changed from being 'Soul of the Sea' to 'Reaching New Lands' and also a piece I wrote yesterday."

"You wrote a piece of music yesterday? How could you? You didn't have time."

"I did. After you left me to go to your women's meeting, I managed to write a new piece."

"You're unbelievable, Max. What's it called?"

"I can't tell you."

Without warning, Lily jumped on him and threw him down onto the grass verge, then climbed on top of him and held him down and tickled him. Max went bright red. He had never laughed so much with another person in his life. It just felt so natural, as if it were meant to be. He couldn't explain why they seemed to have a connection that felt deeper than having just met. He felt as if he had known her for a long time.

"Tell me the name of your new composition or I won't stop tickling you until you're crying."

Max tried to push her off, but his arms were weak from laughter. His sides were aching, and he couldn't think straight. "Okay, okay, I give in."

"Tell me, or I'll start again."

Max opened his mouth then closed it again.

"*Tell me.*" She pushed her hands under his armpits.

"No, stop, please stop, I'll tell you."

Lily sat on top of him, her fingers poised to attack him again.

Max composed himself. "I hope you are okay with this but I sort of used your name."

"What do you mean, sort of used my name?"

"I called my composition 'Lily' after our walk yesterday. You said you would go to the dance with me tonight, by which I think you were saying that you were my girlfriend."

"I did not. I said Eliot asked to be my boyfriend. I only

asked you to the dance." She smiled. "Did ycu really name it Lily?"

The bottom fell out of Max's world. "I did, I'm sorry I thought you meant..."

"Ha, I'm joking, of course, you're my boyfriend! I wish you had asked me on the coach here. We head back in a few days. We need to go for long walks and have time together for kissing and to swap addresses."

Max had stopped concentrating when she said kissing.

"Quick, Max, go and play your audition and show them you're the best here. And for some extra inspiration, try this."

Lily hugged him and kissed him on the cheek. She watched as he headed off to fetch his violin.

14

THE ASSESSMENT

Max walked into the practice room where Edward Parks and two of the other mentors sat waiting for him. This time Mr Parks sat facing his pupil. "Good morning, Max. I assume you have already met Mr Crichton and Ms Bartholomew."

Max nodded.

"I requested you play the piece 'Soul of the Sea' from the other day and also a second piece of your choice. Have you come prepared?"

"Yes, sir. Although I have changed the first piece's name to 'Reaching New Lands'. It's based on my arrival here from England."

Mr Parks nodded and Max laid out his scribbled notation on his music stand and placed it in the middle of the room. He positioned his violin on his shoulder and checked the tuning, then closed his eyes and took a few deep breaths.

"I'm ready."

"Okay, Max, in your own time."

Once again Max sought out his first encounter on the river. It took him the first few bars before he was back and lost within it. Once more the waves crashed around him, and he lost all sense of where he was. With his eyes closed, he didn't see the mentors' expressions of surprise. They took copious notes all the way until Max's bow dragged across the strings with the final note. He fell silent and opened his eyes. He could see them clapping at his performance, but the sound was muted. Max remained silent outwardly but was still present in the beautiful world he had escaped into, the music still playing in his head far more powerful and beyond what he had played. He realised there was still far greater music to be brought out from his river experience.

"Have you ever heard such talent from such a young player?" Mr Parks asked the others.

Ms Bartholomew regarded the young man before her. "Where did you get this piece from, Max? Have you found some old manuscript in a music library? This performance is way beyond my expectations."

"No, Ma'am. I wrote this piece the day after I arrived here. It isn't finished yet; in my head I have another three sections still to add."

"You intend to make this part of a bigger piece?" Mr Crichton frowned. "I wouldn't do that. Keep it as a solo piece; it feels perfect to me as it is."

"I would like to extend it, sir; I have ideas for the other parts."

Mr Parks observed his student. Max was capable when being questioned and didn't just agree with the teachers; he answered as he saw fit. He liked that trait in the young musician.

"Max, your second piece today is, hopefully, another piece of beautiful music, but this time without a name."

"No name yet, sir, as I only composed it yesterday. For now, I'll call it 'Argyll' since we're here in Scotland."

"Excellent." The assessors sat waiting as Max prepared to play his second piece.

He closed his eyes and thought of Lily. He plucked a carefree rhythmic part that felt full of fun. His bow played a slow, hypnotic dance, fed by the music in his head and his violin. His movements were clearly defined as he chased the notes in his head. He didn't need to read his music; he only had to follow the imagery of Lily. Every thought created a distinct picture of her, imprinted on his mind forever.

As he played, images of her streamed through his head like one of the great classic movies. He saw her hair blowing wildly in the wind as they walked along the beach. He could smell her perfume on his skin; he could feel her warmth, her eyes dancing, as she teased him.

The imagery grew stronger and forced Max to change melody and perform at a more powerful volume. He could feel Lily, her sense of freedom as she sat on top of him, tickling him, her body soft and warm as she pressed against him.

The virtuoso musicians watched in silence, stunned at what they were witnessing.

Max played on, his head lost, delighting in everything that was Lily, her exuberance and effervescence. He ran his bow up through every note, building to the ultimate peak of happiness. He had achieved something he didn't know was possible. He watched as the images and notes played on.

But now he was going the wrong way – sadness was overtaking his piece, his distress evident as she left him. Lily walked away from the coach; her head bent down to the ground. How would life feel without her? His bow moved slowly, painfully and without a note of pleasure. He didn't want to feel this part, inevitable as it was. He saw himself back home, collapsed and heartbroken. His life would never be the same again. He quietly drew his tune to an end.

Max opened his eyes, surprised at the scene before him.

There was silence. No clapping, no reaction. It couldn't have been good enough. The mentors seemed in shock. Tears streamed down Ms Bartholomew's face, an emptiness in her eyes.

She was the first to speak. She tried hard to formulate her words, struggling through her grief. "What secrets have you learnt, young man? Where does this music come from? My assessment is it is not of this world and certainly not written by a fourteen-year-old boy. Somehow, you have managed to tune into the very essence of life itself. What other musician has ever given such joy and absolute emptiness to their audience in one tune?"

Max eyed the doorway. He too felt the overwhelming emotion and wanted nothing more than to run to his room and hide.

"Where has this talent come from, Max? You have to come to France to study with my orchestra. We can help nurture a talent like yours. I promise you: we will have every top musician at your disposal."

The statement threw Max. *Why would I be given top musicians?* he wondered.

Mr Crichton sat back in his chair, staring up at the high ceilings. He shook his head as he tried to understand the previous ten minutes of his life. "I'm wiped out, son. My body and mind cannot take any more of what you played. I'm not even sure what style you were playing. I started off by watching you, to observe your playing, your technique. But then my emotions took over and I could no longer concentrate. To sum it up, if that is possible, I will say it was beautiful, perfect and yet desolate, heartbreaking and painful. I believe I need time to recover. If you continue to play and make others feel as I do now, then I would suggest you try to end on a happier note. If you don't, you will leave your audience in a similar state of despair." He turned to Max's mentor. "We need to talk later, Mr Parks." At that Mr Crichton stood and left the room, Ms Bartholomew following close behind.

Max wasn't sure how to feel. "Did I do something wrong, sir?"

"No, Max, nothing wrong, you played perfectly. It was a moving piece, but you can't call it 'Argyll'. It was a story of love and heartbreak if ever there was one. Name your piece after someone, or call it something with the word love in it."

Max nodded to his teacher. He placed his violin into his case. Mr Parks helped him clear up and picked his music up for him.

"How could you play from those scribbles, Max? Your composition is not clear or written in proper notation the way a great musician would write it."

"For me, music is more about how it should be played and not how it's written."

"That's true; I get it. But how can you pass your music on to others to play? No one could play from this."

"I'm not sure I could either, sir. I think it's only for me to play."

"No, Max, the beauty of music is in its sharing. You need to let others adopt your work." Mr Parks peered at the name on top of Max's scribbles and smiled. "'Lily'. Ah! That is a far better title than 'Argyll'. Now your music makes sense."

Max's face was crimson. "Please don't tell anyone, sir."

"I don't do tittle-tattle, Max. Your secret is safe with me."

15

ON THE BEACH

As Lily and Max headed towards the beach with the rest of the students, they could see the others already there in the darkness, a fire blazing through the trees. They had just completed their lessons in Scottish country dancing and it had been a riot.

"Good musicians don't necessarily make good dancers," Lily said.

"What are you trying to say about my dancing, Lily?"

"Nothing. I think having two left feet is a thing of joy you should celebrate."

Max grinned. "I know, I'm hopeless at it."

"I wouldn't say hopeless – if you could get your co-ordination, rhythm and steps in the correct order, you'd do okay," she said, breaking into a sprint as Max chased her along the beach.

Someone played the flute, and a side drum kicked in, marking time. They marched in time to the beat towards the shore.

The fire was huge and lit up the faces of the students

standing around it. A separate fire had a barbecue on it, and the smell of chicken and sausages wafted over the beach.

Lily held firmly onto Max's hand. "Look at the stars, Max, this is the best place ever. I don't want to go home on Sunday."

"Me neither. I don't know what we are going to do."

They walked along the beach, away from the others. Many of the students were now playing rounders. An orchestra of sorts was beginning to find its way through the still night.

Lily led Max over the rocks so they were out of sight. She hugged him hard, tears forming in the corners of her eyes.

"Don't cry. We'll work something out."

"We can't, Max. It'll be too difficult. I don't want our time together to end. As soon as you get home, all the girls where you live will be chasing you."

"Don't be silly; girls and me don't go. Honestly, I'm too strange. I'm not exactly a great catch against guys who play rugby or guitar. What girl would want to go out with a violinist?"

"I would."

Max studied her face. He wanted to stay with her more than anything. "When I get home, I'll tell all the girls I'm spoken for. I'll tell them about this crazy girl called Lily-Anne."

"Don't you dare. Take that back or I'll tickle you again. It's Lily, Mr Maximus."

"Hey, that's not my name, it's not Maximus."

"Well, maybe it's time I got the full story. I've been told by teachers Max is usually short for Maxwell or maybe Maxim – could it be either of those?"

They were interrupted when a couple of boys came climbing over the rocks and stopped above them.

"What are you two up to?"

"Nothing," said Max. "We're just talking."

"Oh yeah, right. I think you two are up to no good."

Max didn't like the boy, he only knew him as the trumpet player. "Leave us alone."

"Or what?" said the second boy, whom Max recognised from a quartet.

Lily stood up and grabbed the trumpet player by the neck. "Or if you don't leave now, the others will see you get a beating from a girl. How embarrassing going home with my nail scratches down your face."

The boys backed off. "They're kissing," they yelled before running back towards the campfire.

"I can't believe you just said that," said Max. "And what would you have done if he had wanted to fight?"

"He wouldn't. He was too scared; I could see it in his eyes. I would have smacked him anyway if he annoyed me any more."

"Wow!"

"Why?"

"I'm just surprised you said it. Now I'm scared of Lily the boxer."

"Never mind all this stuff, we don't have much time. We've only one full day tomorrow, and then we're away first thing the following day." She leaned towards him, her lips wet and cold, and kissed him.

He wrapped his arms around her as they both felt a softness they had never felt before. It was heaven. Max took a breath.

"Am I doing it right?"

"Yes, Max, perfect. Do it again, please."

Max could feel her body as she squeezed against him. His head was being taken over by the music again and he tried to stop it. He wanted this moment for himself.

He touched her lips with his tongue and Lily drew back.

"What do you think you're doing?"

"Sorry, I didn't mean it, it sort of just happened."

"Oh my God, do it again."

Max kissed Lily again and touched her lips with his tongue again. Lily replied with hers. All Max could see in his head were fireworks. He had never felt anything like this before.

A girl appeared above them. "Lucky sods," she said watching them. "You better get back, or there'll be no food left. I've been told to come and get you."

They scrambled to their feet and climbed the rocks, following the girl back to the fire. The other students greeted them with claps and whistles. Max went bright red and stared at his feet. Lily smiled and gave a bow. She didn't seem to care what they thought.

A quartet started up, giving backing to the campfire singing.

16

A VISIT TO THE LIGHTHOUSE

Students dragged logs, branches and driftwood along the beach and piled it onto the fire. There was enough wood stacked there to burn all night. A few inquisitive students headed to the lighthouse, intrigued by stories they had heard about the elderly keepers. Max watched the beam of light circle the surrounding area and disappear into the distant darkness.

Loveable loony, Lizzie, from Lily's dorm, headed towards them.

"Hey, are you going to the lighthouse? It's awesome."

"No Lizzie, I've heard too many weird stories about it."

"Honestly, Lily, whatever you do, don't miss it. The old man and woman are so sweet, and guess what?"

"What?"

"They told me I'm going to be famous."

"That's good, Lizzie. How do they know?"

"I'm not sure. But I believed them."

"What do you think, Max? Do you want to visit the lighthouse?"

"I'd rather go for another walk with you if that's okay."

Lily nodded.

"It's up to you." Lizzie shrugged. "The lighthouse remains open late tonight, so anyone who wants to visit, can."

"We'll think about it."

Max took Lily's hand. "Let's go."

"Oh, to be in love," said Lizzie. "I wish I had a boyfriend. I never get one, and I go to every camp. Not one guy has asked me out on this trip. Do I look that bad?"

Lily laughed. "You need to learn how to ask one out like I did with Max."

"You never!"

"She did." Max smiled. "I'm a bit shy, so it was all up to Lily."

Lily laughed. Max caught that mischief in her eyes again, he loved to see it.

"Next camp I go to, I'm asking every guy until one says yes."

"Don't be silly, you can't do that. I'll give you some tips when I get back to our dorm later."

"Awesome, that's what I need. Don't be too late back." Lizzie ran up the path towards the house.

"Thank God she's gone. Now let's find somewhere quiet; I've forgotten what your kiss is like. I think I need a reminder."

"Me too," said Max.

Holding hands, they strolled along the shore, the waves brushing up the pebble beach. The lights from two small yachts followed each other through the dark, heading across to the Isle of Bute. They sat down on the sand, watching the moon.

"Doesn't this make you feel really small?" asked Lily.

"What does?"

"The moon, the water, the Scottish hills – we're so small compared to all of these things surrounding us."

"We are, but I don't think about it."

They heard laughing and saw the lighthouse door open. Three boys came out with the old man and woman waving to them.

"Get yourself into the lighthouse, Max, it's incredible. The old man lets you use the searchlight."

"It's not a searchlight, Jack, it's a fixed lamp," said Max.

"No, it's not. Tell him."

The other two boys looked at Max. "He's telling the truth. When you shine the lamp upwards you can catch the light from the stars."

"Don't be silly. Look at the beam – it just circles."

"Not when you are inside, it doesn't. We were chasing stars. It was amazing."

"Sounds like the old man's been tricking you three."

"Go in and try it. You won't believe how amazing it is inside."

"I don't want to go," said Lily. "I'd be scared."

"I'll come back with you both," said a boy called Nathan. "I promise you it's fun. They told me I was going to be really talented on keyboards."

"What are they, fortune tellers? I think you're losing it, Nathan, how could they possibly know what you will be?"

"I know it sounds improbable, but they took me on a journey tonight and seemed to know a lot about me. I think you should visit."

"I would like to see inside the building and to watch the lamp at the top." Max looked at Lily. She nodded. "Okay, Nathan, lead the way."

"Can I accompany you tomorrow on piano, Max? One of the teachers said you were special. Said your tunes blew his mind." Nathan looked at Lily. "He said your latest composition was called 'Lily'."

"Did he? Well, he shouldn't have. It was a private meeting, and he had no right to discuss it."

"Sorry, I didn't mean to start anything, it's just they were all talking about you. The word 'genius' was used, a lot."

Max raised his eyebrows towards Lily.

Nathan knocked on the door. It opened promptly, revealing an elderly couple. Their skin was like leather as if weathered by years of living near the water.

"Back again so soon, Nathan? Have you forgotten something?" the old woman asked.

"No. I've brought two more for you to convert."

"Oh good. Bring them in. We were expecting them."

Nathan led them in and headed straight back out the door. "I'll see you both tomorrow for practice, and you can tell me what happens to you tonight."

Max stepped inside the door and stood close to Lily. They were indeed an odd couple. *Maybe the rumours are true,* he thought, *they do seem as if they are a hundred years old.*

"What's your name, dear?" the old woman asked.

"It's Lily."

"And what would you like to be when you grow up, Lily?"

Lily thought the question was silly, the sort of thing you would ask a five-year-old. "I'm not sure. Hadn't really thought about it yet. I'll wait to see my exam results and then choose something."

"I'm sure you'll do well whatever you decide, dear." The old man stretched out his hand. "I'm Tom, and this is my wife, Maisie. We're the lighthouse keepers."

Max and Lily shook hands with them. Max looked around the lighthouse and thought it was really cool. There were cases of bottles stacked high at the bottom of the stairs under the coat hooks. As the stairs wound up, so did a spiral shelf covered in bottles. The place felt homely. Max liked it and wondered why all the talk about the lighthouse keepers had been about them being scary. They were anything but.

"I'm Max."

"Welcome to our lighthouse, son. And what would you like to be when you grow up?" Maisie asked.

"I hope this doesn't sound as if I'm boasting, but I really would like to be one of the best violinists ever."

"Why not? It's good to know what you want." Maisie took Max to the crates and searched through them. "Pick a bottle you like – you too, Lily."

They didn't want to question why and went along with the old couple, both selecting a bottle. Maisie peeled off new labels from a sheet and added them to the front of the bottles. She wrote their names on them and the date, and on Max's label she wrote *World-Class Violinist*. Max smiled.

"C'mon Lily, tell me what you really want to be," Maisie persisted.

Lily couldn't think.

"What about love – would you like love in your life?"

Lily looked at Max and nodded. "Definitely. I want to be happy and have kids, with someone who'll love me forever." Maisie wrote the word love on her bottle.

"Okay, up the stairs the both of you, let's see if we can help you achieve what you want in life."

They climbed the winding staircase. Max loved it. He stared at all the bottles on the shelves as they wound their way up. All shapes, sizes and colours, each bottle had someone's name written on it along with their greatest wish.

They stopped momentarily at the first landing where the area opened up into a library. The bookshelves looked fantastic, curved, following the shape of the lighthouse. Max was taking deep breaths and wheezing a little by then. He wondered how the old couple managed the climb so effortlessly.

They continued up again until they reached the next level. Once again it opened up, and there was a bed with two bedside lamps. It looked really cosy.

"I didn't realise you lived in here."

"Oh, we don't. Well, sometimes we do. Depends what's happening out there on the water. Most of the year we sleep in the cottage attached to the lighthouse. On wild and windy nights, we stay up here to make sure we guide any ships away from the rocks. We take it in turns to sleep."

"I think that's awesome. I would like to be a lighthouse keeper."

"Will I change the label on your bottle or will we stick to music, Max? Let's try and help you achieve becoming the best violinist in the world."

They climbed the last of the stairs up into the viewing platform at the top of the lighthouse. The lamp turned, sending out its beam of light and sweeping from one part of darkness to the next. Binoculars of various sizes were stacked along the window ledges.

Max loved being up at the very top of the lighthouse and only wished it was daylight to better see the view.

The old man pulled on a lever. Below the centre of the lamp, a strange looking harness dropped down, floating in mid-air.

"What's that for?" Max asked.

"You'll see in a minute, son. When I say the word, climb into the front of the harness. Make sure you do it at the same time as I do, so we don't lose our balance and fall down the stairwell. It's happened to me a few times, and it is not a pleasant experience."

"You are kidding, aren't you?" Max asked. "I'm not climbing in there, it doesn't look safe."

"I'll do it," said Lily.

"Well done, my darling, it's good to see someone with a bit of spirit."

The old man held on to a rail and stretched his leg over to the harness, instructing Lily to do the same at the front. She leaned over, her leg outstretched, and Maisie shouted for them both to jump. They both leapt and landed in the harness together. Max nearly had a heart attack, thinking of Lily falling down the stairwell. She waved to him, and he waved back. It looked as if they were in World War II plane as pilot and co-pilot, hanging below in the harness.

"What do we do now?" Lily asked.

"Where's your bottle?" Tom asked her.

"She's left it here," said Maisie. "I'll get it." The old woman leant over the edge with the bottle. Her arm was stretched as far as she could reach. Max felt queasy at the thought of this little old lady plummeting to her death. He wanted to offer to do it but was scared of heights himself. Maisie stretched that final bit and screwed the bottle under the centre of the lantern.

"You're okay to go now, Tom," she shouted.

The old man pulled some ropes, spinning them around. Lily was laughing. Max was surprised at her bravery.

"Can you see the target up front, Lily?" Tom asked.

"Yes, what's it for?"

"While I steer the light, you need to get that target to focus in on the planet Venus. You said you were looking for love and if we can't find it on Venus, then where will we? Venus should have more than enough for you."

"I wouldn't know which planet is which. How can I point it to Venus if I don't know which light in the sky it is?"

"What do they teach you young ones in school nowadays? Look at the map of stars in front of you, Lily. Try and match them up with what you can see in the night sky."

The harness spun around, throwing them from side to side. Lily screamed and laughed as she held on tight. She cross-checked her map with the sky, trying to find a match. It was hard to keep focused. Eventually, she spotted the pattern and made a match. "I've found it!"

"Set the target with Venus in the middle," Tom shouted.

"I've got it. What do I do now?"

"Is your bottle in place under the lamp?"

"Yes."

"Okay, press the button above the bottle and let's see if we can capture some light from this planet of love."

Lily pressed the button and looked out of the window in front of her. She could see the lighthouse beam sweep across the sky towards Venus and hold still on the planet. A reddish pinkish beam of light shot down, travelling towards the lighthouse beam.

"How does your bottle look?" the old man shouted.

"Just the same," said Lily, only to look again and see it glowing pink. "It's turned pink! How did that happen?"

"Well done Lily, your aim was spot on. You caught some light from Venus. Close the top of the bottle for now and whatever you do, don't fall off the cradle."

Lily lifted the bottle off the lamp holder and screwed the top on. Inside the bottle, the light swirled around in pinkish clouds. She stood up, holding her bottle while keeping her balance. Max leaned over the balcony and held out his hand to help her. He pulled her back onto the platform. All week he had stared at her face, but tonight her smile seemed broader than ever. Her cheeks flushed red with excitement.

"Was that fun?" Max asked.

"That was the best. I didn't know what I was doing, but I loved it."

Maisie came up beside them. "It will all make sense when Max has caught his light, I promise. Go on, Max, over you go."

Max looked at the harness. He didn't want to look frightened in front of Lily and so climbed over the edge of the balcony. He stretched his foot out as far as he could but was still short by a couple of feet.

"Jump," Tom urged him.

Max froze. "I'm not sure I can make it. I'm scared I'll fall."

"You'll be fine, Max. I did it. Just jump the last bit, it's perfectly safe."

"I can't." Max looked at the old man sitting waiting in the harness.

"It's all about belief, son. Trust yourself. If we were outside on the ground, you could jump three feet no problem – maybe even six feet. All that has changed is the height you stand at, but it is still only three feet. I did it, and I have far less flexibility than you. Believe in yourself, Max, don't let anything stand in your way. This is the smallest of hurdles, and you say you want to be the world's greatest violinist. You'll have bigger steps than this to take if you want to get to the top. I believe in you and so do the girls."

Max turned round to see Lily and Maisie nodding.

"Do it, Max, I believe in you," Lily said. "Do it for yourself or if you want, do it for me. I want to see you catch the light."

Max leapt from the balcony and landed in the cradle, almost crushing the old man. "I did it!"

"You did indeed. Well done. Now, let's look for Mars."

"Why Mars?"

"Mars has everything you need to be the best. The Romans call it the God of War but others have said Mars represents intuition and habits. Its light can carry inner drive, stamina and confidence. You're going to need all of these attributes if you want to be world class. Without them, you'll never make the grade."

"Are you saying if we point our target at Mars we are going to receive all these things into this bottle?"

"Possibly. It depends on how good your aim is."

Max placed his bottle below the lamp and fixed it in place. He studied the map of stars in front of him and the position of the one coloured red, then looked up at the sky, comparing the stars. He started to swing the cradle round. The old man lay back and let Max take full control. Max found the controls sensitive and realised why Lily had been laughing so much. It was fun swinging back and forth, but it was also slightly frustrating. He glanced back at Lily. Her expression spoke volumes without words; he knew what she meant and stared back at her. Lily raised her eyebrows and smiled at him, filling his head with music once again.

With the music and the cradle both in tune, Max swung the device round in slow motion. The old man knew Max was in control now, as the whole situation felt more stable than the earlier jostling he had experienced with Lily.

Max lined his eyeglass up with Mars. He could see the planet giving off the red glow. Max watched the beam of the lighthouse point upwards almost to twelve o'clock as Mars was directly above. He wondered what the locals and any passing ships would think was happening inside the lighthouse. Holding the target fixed on Mars, he pressed his button, watching the beam trace through the night sky. His eyes were firmly on the beam, wanting to know what this couple were doing to make the bottles glow the way they did. But his bottle was still dark. He glanced up again at Lily, who blew him a kiss and mouthed "I love you." Max's pulse raced, and the most beautiful love song played in his head.

"Wake up, son, you've done it."

Max felt the tapping on his shoulder. He looked at his bottle, and it was bright red, glowing with the strangest light.

"I missed it. I was watching so closely I never saw the light appear."

"It's okay. I think your mind was elsewhere, with your girlfriend."

"She's not my..."

"Oh really? I've not felt that much love in this room for a long time. You don't need to explain. Now let's get out of this cradle, I'm tired."

Tom climbed up and leaned over, grabbing the bottom rail of the balcony and pulling himself up. Once again, Max was surprised how fit the old man was. He stood up and was unsteady trying to balance.

"Just lean over and trust yourself," Maisie said.

Max handed his bottle over then leaned over and grabbed the rail. Lily pulled him up and gave him a hug.

"I felt tremendous after that, what about you, Max?"

"Same. Once I focused on Mars, I felt as if I were joined to that machine."

"Okay you two, come over here," said Maisie as she

walked around the top of the lighthouse lamp. They followed her and stopped in front of the big lens.

"Did you enjoy chasing stars and finding the planets that will give you special powers through capturing the light?"

"It was fun," said Lily. "I didn't know what I was doing, but I enjoyed it."

Max nudged her. "And I heard that you said you would never come to this lighthouse because of the two strange old keepers in it."

"No, I didn't mean that. I – "

"It's okay sweetheart, we hear it all the time. Now then, Lily, I want you to open your bottle carefully and breathe as much of the light in through your nose. If there's any left in the bottle after that, I want you to drink it. That is, if you want what you said, to be loved."

"I do, I want lots of love in my life." Lily opened her bottle, and a wisp of pink light slowly unfurled. She put the bottle under her nose and breathed in deeply. Max watched the light streaming up her nose. Afterwards, Lily's bottle was still half full.

"Go on," said Tom, "drink the remainder."

Lily put the bottle to her lips and tipped her head back. Max saw the bottle go dark. It was back to being an ordinary bottle again. Lily looked content, her eyes staring at Max dreamily. She looked slightly drunk.

"Now you, son, remind me first what you want to be."

"I want to be one of the best violinists in the world."

"Excellent, that's entirely possible if you want it. But before you drink this light and feel its incredible powers, I need to ask if you are certain this is what you really want?"

"I'm positive."

"I'm sure you are, Max, but being the best won't happen

simply by taking this. It means lots of hard work. What we have here will only help you so far. The rest has to come from you. Can you put the effort in, the amount needed to be the world's best?"

"Whatever it takes. I'm confident I can."

"Okay, Max. I want you to look at that beautiful light in your bottle. When you inhale this light that's travelled millions of miles from Mars to Earth, it will give you power beyond your dreams. To be the best in your chosen career you'll need stamina, for those moments when you are too tired and want to give up. I need you to think of this light inside you, lighting up your head and giving you the strength you need to carry on. It will also provide you with confidence, more than enough of it."

"I understand."

"If others put you down, look inwards for confidence. You will be served with an abundance of the light, more than enough for one person. This light will keep you focused on the long road ahead of you. Go on, Max, open your bottle, you know the drill."

Max opened his bottle. The light inside seemed more active than Lily's, almost bubbling to get out. He placed it under his nose and breathed in. He could feel the light enter his head. Coloured shapes danced in front of him, swirling in all directions: he had never felt this good before. His eyes widened. This was like nothing he'd ever experienced. Sparks flew in front of his eyes. When he could inhale no more, he stopped as he was feeling slightly giddy. The bottle still had plenty in it. Max lifted the bottle to his mouth and drank in the light. This time he couldn't feel anything. He looked at the bottle again. There was still half the bottle left, so he threw his head back once more, drinking the light. To his surprise, the bottle still had plenty in it even after he finished his second gulp.

The old man smiled at Max and at his bottle. "I think we've got more light in that one than we bargained for. Don't take any more just now, son, or you'll go all dizzy."

Max's face was a picture, grinning from ear to ear. He looked slightly drunk.

The old woman pulled a bag of balloons out of a drawer. She gave one to the old man. Tom put the balloon over the bottle, and it inflated, filled with the yellow glowing light. He tied the balloon. But the bottle had yet more in it. He put a second balloon on and filled that too. Maisie tied the balloons together with string and handed them to Max. They were extraordinary: balloons glowing with light.

The bottle was back to normal, empty with only his name, the year and *World-Class Violinist* written on the label.

"You can untie the balloons later and take in as much light as you can."

Max nodded to the old man.

Maisie came forward and took the bottles from them both.

"Can I keep my bottle?" Max asked.

"Afraid not. We'll put it on the shelf, and one day when you come back as a successful musician, you can see it again."

Max smiled. By the time he achieved what he wanted, he wasn't sure these two would still be alive.

Tom pulled a cord in the roof, turning off all the lights at the top except the lamp. They descended the stairs, and halfway down Maisie placed their bottles on the shelf. They were the last two bottles on the spiral. They climbed further down until they were at the bottom entrance hall.

Tom shook their hands and Maisie gave them a hug. "Follow your dreams and don't let this be a wasted night," she said. "Seize life with both hands and make it work for you. Believe that you can change the world for the better."

Lily and Max nodded.

"Will you come back and play for me one day, Max?" Maisie continued. "I would like to hear you."

"Sure. I'm not sure I'll know how to get here, but I'll do my best."

"You'll find us, I'm sure. And Lily, don't forget to give your love. Many people are starved of love in this world. Give as much as you can."

"I will."

The lighthouse door closed behind them, leaving them standing in the dark of the night. The two balloons floated high above them, lighting their path.

"What just happened there?" Lily asked Max.

"I have no idea!" He giggled. "I think they are a bit cuckoo. All that stuff about catching light."

"I liked them. It felt real."

"So did I, Lily, but how did that light get into those bottles and how did we manage to breathe it in or drink it?"

"I don't know. Did you taste or feel anything?"

"I felt a bit funny."

"Me too. I felt a surge of love, as if I wanted to run around and hug everyone."

"You can hug me if you want."

They walked towards the beach, where the fire was still burning. Teachers and students sat around, telling stories. Max and Lily sat together, holding hands and listening to the fireside tales, the balloons bumping together in the breeze.

"I feel as if I'm floating through the air with those balloons."

"I don't want to go home, Max. I don't ever want to leave you."

Max pulled Lily towards him and hugged her. She kissed his neck, moving slowly round to his lips. They held each other silently for a while, before heading back to the castle.

"We've got the journey home together," said Max. "Then we need to arrange how we can meet up. We can call and write to each other until we can get together properly."

"Are you asking me to be your girlfriend once we get home, Maximus?"

Max smiled at her name calling and nodded. "Yes, I think I am."

They kissed in the hallway, scared to let each other go, both fearful of what little time they had left together.

One of the team leaders came past. "Okay, you two, time to head to your rooms. Most of the others are in bed, and the lights are going out."

For the first time, Max saw uncertainty in Lily's eyes.

They headed to their dormitories. Max tied his balloons onto the end of his bedpost. He turned off the light and lay back, watching the balloons gently bump off each other, their light casting a yellow glow around his bed. He looked up the dormitory to see if anyone wanted to talk but everyone was asleep.

What happened to us tonight?

Max grabbed the string from one of the balloons and pulled it down. He untied the knot and let the light inside slowly flow into his mouth. It didn't taste of anything but he started to get light-headed again. The balloon let out a high pitched squeak as it gave up the last of its contents and lay deflated. Max started laughing, burying his face into the pillow so as not to wake anyone. All the others remained asleep. He tapped the other balloon back and forth, deciding he would leave it until morning before taking the rest of its light. He tapped it again and the balloon broke free from its string. It climbed high towards the old rafter beams, where it became stuck.

Max padded across the room in his bare feet and stood below the rafters. Picking up a pair of balled socks, he threw them hard towards the balloon to dislodge it but instead he burst it. The light showered down on top of him like raindrops.

"What the hell are you up to, Bruford?" one of the boys mumbled, looking up from his bed.

"Nothing," said Max. "Go back to sleep."

He made his way back to his bed still covered in beads of light. He rubbed them into his skin; his body looked luminous. He got into bed and kept checking under the covers to see himself still glowing.

What a crazy night.

17

THE JOURNEY HOME

Lily and Max sat on the rocks watching the sunrise. It was cold, the river had not one ripple. The hills reflected in the perfect mirror image. The young lovers didn't talk much. Lily squeezed his hand.

"We'll be okay; we'll arrange to meet up once we're home," she said.

"I don't want to go home. I can't face not seeing you."

"Same."

Lily leaned over and cuddled into Max. They wrapped their arms around each other, their kissing becoming more passionate.

"Let's run away," said Lily.

Max smiled. He loved her adventurous spirit. She wasn't frightened of anything. "That would be good, but I don't think we would last long on a few pounds. I'll talk to Mum and arrange for you to come to London. I can show you the sights."

They watched the sun rise above the water.

"We'd better get back before they send out a search party."

The students gathered in the main hall with their instruments in hand. There was a buzz of excitement as they prepared to play their last concert before packing up for home.

Ms Falconer arranged the orchestra into position then, just as she had on the first day, she raised her arms and lowered them slowly, achieving silence from the students. "Right! We are finally getting somewhere," she announced. "When working in an orchestra, learn to prepare with no talking or clattering of music stands. You are professionals. Be quiet, calm, tune your instrument and sort your music before you take your place."

She paused as Mr Parks and the other virtuosos entered the room and looked over the students who seemed to have grown up over the last ten days.

"Today you'll go home changed people. Who you are now is different to who you were when you arrived here. There have been some remarkable discoveries amongst you; this is part of our reason to host the retreat to discover exceptional talent.

"What we hope you've learnt is how to better yourselves in the bigger music community out there. You have the power to change and improve any orchestras you play with. Go back home and show your friends and family how worthwhile this week has been for you."

More teachers and volunteers filtered in, taking their seats in front of the orchestra in readiness of them playing. Ms Bartholomew and Mr Parks joined Ms Falconer on stage.

"Over the week you'll have learnt your part in Ms Bartholomew's composition, 'Going Home,'' Ms Falconer continued. "But before we play, three students are to be recognised for outstanding performances. On cello, can we have a big round of applause for ... Orla Wright."

The students bounced their bows off their instruments, and the percussionist played a small run on the xylophone. Orla took a bow as she picked up her certificate. Max glanced at Lily sitting behind her own cello. She was strangely quiet.

"On percussion, let's hear it for Rowanna Taylor for her skills on five different instruments."

The students cheered as the girl went up to collect her certificate.

"And finally, the star pupil this year for both playing ability and composition is..."

Max looked around the room, sure he knew who would win this. Lily glanced at him and gave him a thumbs-up sign.

"Max Bruford."

Everyone in the room stood and clapped for Max. Whoops and ye-haws sounded from around the room. Max hadn't expected this at all. He stood up and took a bow, raising his violin in the air. He made his way through the crowd to Mr Parks, who shook his hand and presented him with his certificate and a sealed envelope. Max blushed, thinking many of the other students were just as good as he was.

"I'm sure you'll agree with me, each of these students shone in their individual sections amongst their peers. Right, let's get to business before we start to break down, knowing we are all leaving each other soon." Ms Falconer took a small bow and left the stage.

"Quiet, please!" Ms Bartholomew rattled her baton against her music stand. "To the three students awarded certificates, when you reach your part, please take the lead and bring out the best in the rest of us."

The orchestra fell silent. All eyes were on Ms Bartholomew. She lifted her baton and silently counted them in. The low rumble of the timpani sent vibrations across the room as they mimicked the sound of thunder. The orchestra played through the central theme with every member performing at a higher level than when they arrived.

Ms Bartholomew signalled to Max to take the solo spot. He had loved playing this piece in rehearsals, but today it had a significant meaning. He could hear the orchestra in harmony and thought of his mother at the coach park, waiting to welcome him home. She would be excited, desperate to see him again after their first separation. He drew his bow long and low over the strings into a sequence of minor chords. He played along to the imagery lifting his spirit higher. He perfected dragging out the melancholy, soon to be real as Lily headed home, leaving him alone with nothing but beautiful memories.

Max wanted more than memories. He wanted his girlfriend's hands holding him, her arms wrapped around him, her breath on his neck. Without her, the rest of the journey would seem meaningless.

Max was lost in the melody. His heart was hurting with the thought of leaving Lily and it soon became too painful to play anymore. He lifted his bow and let the orchestra play on without him, a fitting ending to honour Lily. Max turned to watch her playing the cello, his stomach dropping at her sad expression. He focused in on her instrument; every note sounded more tragic and more profound than the last.

Ms Bartholomew signalled to Rowanna to come in and

take up her position for the final few bars. Her beaters glided deftly across the xylophone, bringing a bright end to the performance.

The teachers stood up and applauded. They could hear how their guidance had already changed these students in just over a week. The students packed up their instruments and Mr Parks approached Max.

"Make sure you look inside the envelope, Max. Do not throw it away or lose it."

"Why, what's in it, sir?"

"A big surprise, Max. Three different schools of music want you to come and join them. You have three offers of a scholarship to choose from, isn't that wonderful?"

Max could barely speak. Although it was everything he ever dreamed of, he didn't like leaving his mother. If it hadn't been for Lily, he would have felt lonely at Castle Toward.

"It's fantastic, sir. I'll have a look when I get home and talk to my mum and my music teacher and see what they think."

"Max, it doesn't really matter what they think, it's what *you* think that counts. This is what you could call a life-changing opportunity. Do the sensible thing and seize it with both hands."

Max nodded to appease Mr Parks. He needed to decide how much he wanted this and to make a plan to make it happen. They shook hands.

"I'm sure our paths will cross again, Max. You've a lot to offer the world."

Max went to his dormitory and collected his suitcase before heading outside. There were three coaches, two marked for London and one to Aberdeen. Max walked around the back and saw Lily sitting at the window. He approached the driver with his case, but the driver stopped him.

"Sorry son, you're going to have to get on the other coach to London, this one is full."

Max felt sick. He had to sit with Lily; it was their last day. Leaving his case outside, he climbed aboard regardless. The coach was packed with no seats left. A girl sat next to Lily. Max approached her.

"Would you mind travelling on the other coach?"

"Yes, I would. I'm not moving. I'm fine where I am."

"Lily, come off this coach and come on the other."

"I can't Max, I already tried. They said I have to stay on this one."

Max cleared his throat. "Who would like to travel on the other coach?" he shouted. No one answered.

Max went into his wallet and looked at the small amount of money he had left. "I will give seven pounds to anyone who will go to the other coach to London to allow me on here," he called out.

"Max, don't give away all your money," pleaded Lily.

A large boy Max knew only from his nickname 'Slim' came towards him. "Did you say you'll give me seven pounds to travel on the other coach?"

"Yes."

"Let's see it. I don't believe you."

Max pulled the money from his wallet and held it up in front of Slim's face.

"I'll take it."

"Not so fast. You have to get the guy next to you to move over to this seat where Lily is sitting so we can sit together."

"I'm not moving," the other boy said.

"What about you?" Slim addressed the girl next to Lily.

"You move down to my seat."

"No, I'm comfortable where I am."

"I'll give you a pound."

"Two," she said, holding two fingers up.

"Okay, two it is. Move seats."

Max handed over his seven pounds to Slim who handed two to the girl, who pocketed it with glee. As they both set about changing seats, Max jumped off the coach and gave the driver his case, then sat beside Lily. She had been quiet throughout the entire exchange. Now she took his hand and stared out the window.

The engine roared, and the driver started the bumpy ride down the drive. Max held tightly onto Lily.

When they arrived at the ferry, everyone got off the coach like last time. They climbed the steps to the top deck and hugged.

"Are you okay, Lily?"

"No. I've never felt so bad in my life, Max. I know we're young, but I don't want to leave you. I want to stay on the coach all the way to London with you."

"That's what I want too. There must be a way around this. We can write and call, and I can ask my mum to take me to Carlisle for my holidays."

Lily laughed. "She'll thank you for that. Have you ever been to Carlisle? It's not exactly where you would go for a holiday."

"Then we can arrange to go to somewhere like Blackpool or Morecambe and meet up. My mum would get on with your parents, I'm sure."

Lily wrapped her arms around Max. "Don't let me go."

Max hugged her back. They both stared at the water and Max could hear the music in his head once more, a different tune this time, with sadder undertones. Deep down he knew he wouldn't see much more of Lily once he was back, but that didn't change the feeling of wanting her with him always.

They headed back to their seats on the coach as the ferry prepared to dock. Lily didn't say much for the rest of the journey. She knew the driver would be letting her off first and the last thing she wanted was to create a scene. The young lovers hugged and kissed as much as they could. Lily's wish at the lighthouse had been for love, and now she realised it wasn't as she imagined. Love could be painful, and she could feel the pain, deep within.

The driver pulled in at the side of the road. "First stop, Carlisle," he shouted.

Lily stood up. Max went to follow her.

"Don't, Max. My parents will be there, they wouldn't understand. Write to me every day or try and call me on Tuesday night at seven." She kissed him one last time and walked off the coach. Max was on the wrong side and stood up to peer out of the opposite window. He spotted a woman who looked so like Lily she had to be her mother. She was well dressed and had her arm round Lily while the driver fetched her case. They walked away from the coach towards a car. Lily looked back and waved. Half the coach waved back, and Max knew she would never make him out in amongst all these faces.

The coach moved off, and for the first time, Max felt empty. He didn't want to go back home, or play the violin any more, and he didn't care about the stupid offers he'd received in his letter. Only Lily occupied his thoughts. He closed his eyes and wondered why she had picked him. She could have had any guy as her boyfriend and yet she chose him.

He could hear the music he had written for her in his

head. He would need to extend the piece to add in this separation, this emptiness. Then Mr Crichton's words after his assessment came to mind, and Max realised he also needed to bring more joy in the piece so his listeners wouldn't end up broken hearted.

He reached for his notepad and pencil and began to compose. All the different images of Lily, the laughter, the tears – it was all there in the music. Max wrote, scored out and rewrote all the way to London, disembarking the coach only once to get some lunch.

When he at last finished writing, he looked up. London was visible ahead, and he knew he was close to home.

As the coach pulled into the coach park, Max saw his mother waiting. He was surprised to see her, looking smart, dressed in a new outfit with her hair and make-up all in place. Max wondered where she was going.

He got off the coach, but his mother stayed put. She had remembered not to embarrass him in front of the others. He collected his bag and waved to the others on the coach as it drove off.

"Look at you, Max, how you've changed!" His mum wrapped her arms around him. "I missed you so much. I thought you might have called more often."

"I tried, Mum, but we were swamped. We didn't have time to think."

"It's okay, I realised that. The main thing is you enjoyed yourself. You did, didn't you?"

"It was the best time ever. I didn't want to leave."

Mary looked shocked. "You mean you didn't want to come home?"

"No Mum, of course I wanted to come home, but I was having such a fantastic time with my music and other things I wanted to stay. We had campfires down on the beach at night, and I visited a lighthouse, and I made some new friends."

"You can tell me all about it. I've booked a restaurant for our dinner tonight. I assumed you would be hungry after travelling all day."

The last thing Max felt like was going to a restaurant, but he could see all the effort she had gone to. "Let's go, then. I'm starving."

Mary slipped her arm through Max's and led him to the car.

At the restaurant Max told her everything that had happened, everything except Lily. He wasn't sure how she would react to him having a girlfriend. He decided to leave it for now.

"Three offers, Max, that's incredible. Which one do you want to take?"

"I haven't thought about it yet. Let's leave it for now until we talk to Miss Beaton. She will know more about the different schools and offers."

As they ate their dinner, Max began to feel settled again. Being home was good.

III

PRESENT DAY

18

THE RETURN

Max sat up on his bed at the Seafront Hotel. *Time to move on*, he thought, rubbing sleep from his eyes. Such memories achieved nothing more than to torture him about his past. He decided to stop playing it over and over in his head. Today was the day he would exorcise these demons by revisiting the lighthouse and finding out if anyone in the area remembered the old couple and what happened back then.

He left the hotel and headed towards the village of Toward, his head still reeling from the party at the village hall. He enjoyed every second of the walk, breathing in the crisp, clean air. It felt so refreshing. He was sure being in Scotland was cleansing his mind, body and soul.

As he walked, he composed another tune in his head. He couldn't help but hear the echo of bagpipes after the noise in the village hall.

At last, he saw the lighthouse up ahead and the small cottage adjoining it. The building was white and finished with pale green trims around the windows and door frame. As Max approached, he realised it didn't look any different to how he remembered it. A low-level wall separated the building from the seashore.

Feeling an unexpected twist of nerves, Max tried to reason with himself to not to be so ridiculous. He wondered who lived here now and if they knew what took place here all those years ago. Were they fed up of people like him turning up at their door on a nostalgia trip?

Stalling for time, Max surveyed the coastline. He could see rocks sticking out of the water at various points. The Isle of Bute faced him, and in the backdrop mountains rose towards the sky, dark and menacing. *That has to be the Isle of Arran,* he thought.

Plucking up courage, he made his way to the front door of the cottage. He lifted the heavy iron knocker and hit it off the door twice. Nothing, not a sound. He raised the knocker again, but this time with a lot more vigour he hit the door many times. Once again, no answer.

He stepped back from the door and looked up to the top of the lighthouse, where he could see some movement. Someone was cleaning the windows in the turret where the lamp was housed. He could see a hand wiping back and forth across the glass. He walked to the centre of the garden and waved upwards.

At first, nothing happened, and then he saw a face peer down at him, then the hand waved back. Max walked back to the front door and waited. Five minutes later, the door opened.

Max's mouth fell open. Before him stood Maisie, the very same lady he had met as a boy. She looked old, but no older than when he had last seen her.

"Ah," she exclaimed, "Max! You look as if you've just seen a ghost. I get it, you thought I'd be dead, didn't you?"

"Y-yes ... no, I mean no." Max stuttered over his words.

He was taken aback by the sight of the sharp-witted old woman. He had indeed thought she would be long dead but was far more grateful to see she was still alive. "How on earth do you remember my name?"

"Oh, we've been expecting you on and off for the past few years. One minute you're coming, the next you've changed your mind. Not to worry, you are finally here."

Max couldn't speak. The old woman was right: he had arranged to come back a few times, but it never happened. Not his fault entirely, as concerts and recording kept taking precedence. But how would she know?

"That's true. But how do you remember me? I've not been here for a very long time."

"We met the last time you were here. Don't you remember? You said you wanted to be a world-class violinist."

"Yes, I remember, but that was forty years ago! You can't possibly have remembered me or what I told you after forty years. I don't look anything like I did back then."

"I remember every kid that's ever passed through these doors, and what their dreams were. I've got a reminder of them all on the stairwell with the bottles."

Max was stunned. "And what about your husband, Tom, is he still alive?"

"Of course he is. Why, has someone told you differently? Didn't you notice how white the lighthouse is? He's been hanging from a rope and a plank all of last week painting it, knowing you were coming to visit. He's been washing the stairs while I was cleaning the windows. I only stopped to let you in. Come through."

Max gazed at the cottage as he was led through the living area. It was the ultimate in cosy, with mementoes everywhere. Ornaments of all shapes and sizes filled the room. A tree made of thank you cards and pictures of hundreds of students with handwritten messages lined the walls. Max suspected they weren't family but more likely to be pupils who had previously visited.

The coal fire roared in the hearth, giving a warm, dreamy feel to the living area. Max loved the room and could only describe it as organised chaos. With a jolt, he realised how devoid of life his minimalist-style flat was in comparison to the old couple's house.

Tom appeared in the doorway with a bucket and mop in his hands. "Max! How are you? Long time no see." He stretched his arm out towards Max.

Again Max was rooted to the spot. This man looked no different. He spoke as if he had seen him a week ago.

Max cleared his throat. "I'm fine, sir. You're looking well," he said, remembering his manners and stepping forward to shake his hand.

"Can't complain, although my back can't take it like it used to. I'm sick of washing those stairs."

Max grinned at the old man, delighted at the seeming normality of the situation.

"Maisie, would you mind organising a tray of tea and biscuits for our guest and we can hear what Max has to say about his life. The real stuff, not what we've read in the papers."

"The kettle's already on."

"Which papers?" Max asked.

"The newspapers, son. We keep an eye on who's doing what and who has fallen or given up."

Max was struggling with what they were saying. *How could they possibly keep tabs on all these pupils?*

As they sat with tea and biscuits, the odd spark from the fire threw a burning ember onto the rug. Each time Maisie would huff and reach forward to extinguish it. Max decided to surrender to the odd situation and proceeded to explain how his visit to the lighthouse had had a profound, life-changing effect on him.

"I left here feeling as if I had superpowers and spent the next day duelling with a world-class violinist. When I returned home, I practised six hours a day, developing my skills to a level of excellence. My teacher, Miss Beaton, advised me on which offer to accept. With her guidance, I was accepted into one of the most prestigious London schools of music. Once there, I was singled out for having extraordinary talent. I never told them about the light from Mars and the powers you gave me. Twelve months later, I won a nationwide competition for young musicians. I was officially the best in the country."

"We read about that," said Tom, smiling. "We knew you were doing well."

"From then on I played with different orchestras, often as the first violinist. Sometimes I would get a solo spot but nothing notable. It was only when I decided to take my own music on tour that life changed dramatically. One of my symphonies kept me in demand the world over and I played to sell-out crowds across Europe, America, Russia, Australia and Argentina. This was unusual for a youngish classical musician playing their own compositions. I've released four albums that all attained platinum status."

Tom chuckled. "Maisie and I loved that you named your main symphony *The Lighthouse Keepers*. We never really considered it was for us; we saw it as a shout-out to all the lighthouse keepers across the world."

Max couldn't help but shake his head in wonder. They were so selfless.

"To say you influenced and helped me is an understatement. I wrote that piece with you both firmly in mind. It was an experience I could never put into words. But I do think I captured what you do rather well."

"You did, Max. You gave what we do some justice. We play your music whenever we need cheering up."

Max smiled.

"Would you like to go upstairs and revisit the lighthouse? See if it brings back old memories for you?"

"I would love to," said Max.

The old man rose to his feet. "Let's get some dinner first. Cleaning that place has made me ravenous. Maisie, let's make Max a meal he won't forget."

The three of them worked together in the kitchen before they sat eating and chatting long into the night, and it was indeed a night to remember. Outside, the night sky was a flaming red, reflecting off the lighthouse.

19

DINNER AND DANCE

After dinner, Tom got to his feet, satiated. He stood with his back to the fire, heating his legs and rubbing his belly. "That food was fit for a king, Maisie."

"You always say that, Tom."

"He's right," Max agreed. "I can hardly move, it was so filling."

Maisie smiled at them both. She was always happy when a pupil revisited them. "Would you be kind enough to play us a tune, Max? I see you've brought your violin."

"Sure, since I owe it to you two for helping me to become world famous."

He took his violin out of its case. It was the same instrument he had as a boy and his mentor Mr Parks had been right when he said it would get better with age. He had never forgotten the sacrifice his mother had made to buy him his instrument. As soon as his fame brought him wealth, he'd made sure she was comfortable for life, and when she remarried, she was happy once more. Max felt there was no one more deserving.

He picked up his bow and played the third movement of his symphony, 'The Lighthouse Keepers'. The music flowed from his violin, swirling in circles, enchanting and embracing the three of them. The sound was so alive, dancing in and out of every space, filling the room with incredible sounds and light.

As Tom and Maisie danced, they felt wrapped in a cocoon of spiritual melodies, surrounded in a warm glow as the music lifted their spirits higher and higher. They found themselves in a beautiful, heavenly place, floating, encased in love. They held on to each other as Max played, their eyes locked as they each searched the depths of their partner's soul. The feeling was euphoric, and they both wanted more. As the music slowed and all but disappeared, they fell into one another's arms, feeling the same way they did when they first met.

Max caressed the strings until he found the slow, repetitive rhythm to match their heartbeats. Softly, he played on until the notes were barely audible. Eventually, the music fell into silence.

Tom and Maisie collapsed onto the couch. Max removed his bow from his violin and stood in silence, before taking a bow. Tom and Maisie clapped their hands from where they sat.

"How do you do that, Max?" Maisie exclaimed, breathless. "That was undoubtedly the very meaning of love itself. It was the most beautiful music I've ever heard. It's so much better live than listening to your albums. The music is the same, but the power is different."

Tom agreed with his wife. "Why is it so different, Max?"

"Because it has to be experienced, lived in the moment. Recorded music is great but at most a second-best substitute: it can never have the same depth of feeling as live music. I play my music differently to everyone. I play to them personally, based on what I know about them and how I see specific arrangements affect them.

"I feel you have done something to us, Max, something very good," said Tom. "I felt as if I met a higher being tonight."

"That's good. But I think it's I who has to thank both of you for what you gave me."

"Then let's see if we can return the favour, Max. It's time we answered your questions."

"What questions?" asked Max.

"Every person who has ever come back here only returns for one reason, Max: they have unanswered questions they feel they must ask. Are you saying you only came here for tea and biscuits?" Tom smiled.

"Well, now that you mention it, I do need to ask you a few things."

"I thought so. Let's head upstairs to the lamp and see what kind of night it is."

20

CATCHING SOME LIGHT

Max followed Tom and Maisie through the hallway to the bottom of the lighthouse. As they entered, he noticed crates of bottles stacked high. The bottles inside were of many different shapes, colours and sizes. Quite a few looked antique.

Max stared up through the spiral stairwell to the top of the lighthouse. It seemed to go on forever. He thought he could spot the harness hanging below the lamp.

"Now you know why I was so tired earlier," said Tom. "Took me ages to wash those stairs down."

Max grinned. He wasn't sure, even in his fit state, if he could clean that amount of steps. As they climbed the stairs, Max studied the bottles on the shelves. He was fascinated by the different labels: 'Farmer', 'Dancer', 'Singer', 'Live in Australia'. People's dreams were so different. He watched as the shelf followed the curve of the staircase from the bottom, all the way to the top. He remembered his first visit when he was asked to pick a bottle of his own. He looked closer, to see if he could spot it.

As they reached the first landing, Max's breath was

taken away by the sheer beauty of the library. Stepping up from the stairwell, Max gazed in wonder. Although he'd seen it before, he hadn't had an adult's appreciation of its majesty. There were thousands of books, all set in carved ornamental bookcases. Clearly a master craftsman had built the library. Max's memories returned to him as he looked at the books. In the middle of the room were two comfy, well-worn chairs with matching footstools. Beside the bookcases was a large table with books lying open on it. Underneath the table sat a few board games and a chess set. Max ran his fingers along the spines of the books, comparing the different genres. They comprised many subjects: ships of the seas, rescue services, science books, astronomy, UFO sightings, spiritual awakenings, fairies – such a strange and esoteric mix. He walked to the next set of shelves and every book bore a person's name. They appeared to be arranged in no sensible order that Max could make out.

"All the people who have visited us, Max," said Maisie. "It makes for interesting reading."

Max was trying to work out how they got information on everyone. Many of these volumes easily predated the age of the internet. He followed the curve of the shelves with the shape of the building.

"I barely remember this room. Was it like this when I was last here?"

"Yes, it hasn't changed much. We've added more books over the years, and I've had the chairs reupholstered in Royal Stewart tartan."

"They look good."

"Thank you. Apart from that, I don't think we've changed much," said Maisie.

"It looks incredible. The bookcases are a work of art."

"Yes, we were pleased with them," said Tom. "They

were mainly made from driftwood by one of our night visitors who returned. She came back once she had achieved her dream of becoming a master carpenter and helped us build them."

"I'm blown away. She did a fantastic job."

"She did. This is where Tom and I sit and read to keep up to date with our visitors and the world."

Max could picture them both wrapped up warm and poring over their books, the wind howling outside. It was a beautiful space to sit.

Maisie and Tom started up the stairs to the next level. Max read some of the names on the bottles as he passed by. He recognised a few celebrity names of actors and singers. He was privately pleased to know these people had something in common with him. They had all visited the lighthouse and chased the light from distant planets.

The three of them reached the second level, where a bed was visible through a heavy set of velvet curtains. Max recalled how they had told him they sometimes slept at the lighthouse as they needed to keep a lookout on stormy nights, sharing sleeping shifts. "Nice curtains, like the ones I have to go through on stage," he said.

"Thank you," said Maisie. "They keep the heat in; it's freezing otherwise. The draught whistles up the stairs when it's a howler outside."

Max thought it still looked homely.

They carried on up the final flight to the top. Max took in the panoramic view from the windows as he walked round the turret. The sun was reflecting off the clouds, painting them many shades of red and orange, with the corn-blue sky the perfect background. Already the north star stood alone in the light as bright as could be. It wouldn't be long before the sun sank behind the hills, bringing darkness with it, and then the other stars would show themselves. He stood and stared at the beauty of it, his head already filling with music.

Max startled with the realisation he was surrounded by bottles with different coloured light shining from them. Just like before, the harness-style chair made of white canvas hung beneath the central lamp, and a telescope with what looked like a target on top was pointing towards the sky.

The lighthouse keepers sat down on a small bench. Maisie picked up some bottles and started to polish them. "So Max, you have some questions for us?"

"I do, but I don't know where to start."

"At the beginning is always the best place," said Tom.

"I agree, but I'm not sure where the beginning is. All I remember was attending the music retreat along the shore road. We were dared by some of the staff to come down and see the lighthouse."

"And that's what happened, if I remember rightly. You turned up here with a young lady named Lily, and you both wanted to see the lighthouse."

"That's correct. How do you remember Lily's name?"

"Oh, we never forget a visitor."

Max stared at them. He didn't believe they could remember everyone's name who turned up here in the dark. "Lily and I only came to see the lighthouse. We weren't here for the other thing."

"When you say 'the other thing', what do you mean?" said Maisie.

"Up here in the lighthouse ... chasing stars and planets, capturing light and drinking it."

Maisie rocked on her chair in merriment. She raised her hand, laughing as she did so. "Let's correct this story, Max. We made it seem like we were chasing stars and capturing light, but that's not what we were doing. We were just trying to give some children hope to believe in themselves."

"Hope," said Max. "Why hope?"

"Everything we do here is about hope, Max. Helping people believe in themselves," said Tom. "We wanted to help every kid who dreamed of becoming something believe they could do it. It's important to us to let them see someone really believes in them as much as they do themselves, whatever their dream."

"Why's that so important to you?" In the light from the central lamp, Max thought the lighthouse keepers looked quite strange. The conversation wasn't going the way he expected.

"Everyone needs hope, Max. They need to be believed. Not only kids – adults too. That's why more people need to be lighthouse keepers."

"Sorry, I lost you there. What has being a lighthouse keeper got to do with these kids?"

The old man stood up. "Come here." He beckoned to Max.

Max got up and looked out the window.

"Tell me what you see from these windows, Max."

Max stared out into the sunset. The scenery was very special as the sun cast dark shadows across the landscape. "Beautiful hills, the river, stunning views."

"And down below?"

Max looked down. All he could see were the rocks below and some further out. "Rocks," he replied.

"Not just rocks, Max, danger. There are rocks visible above the surface and many more just below the water line that no one can see. Look at the currents, the way the water moves, pulling driftwood and other items. It's dangerous."

"I get it. But I don't know what this has got to do with what we were talking about."

The old man raised his hands to the sky. "Max, when I said more people need to be lighthouse keepers, what do you think I meant?"

"I'm not sure. I thought you just loved your lifestyle and wished more people would live a similar life."

"You are half right. Also, I meant everyone should try and play their part in others' lives by being strong, looking out into the distance to see a new horizon, shining their light to show them the way. And, most importantly, by giving them hope by believing in them and their dreams. Too many people look down at their feet, surrounded by rocks, and give poor advice. They are the dangerous undercurrents pulling and hauling at these young, fertile minds and then dashing their hopes and dreams on the rocks down there. A lighthouse keeper's job is to guide people from the rocks and shine our light into the distance, showing them the horizon is theirs for the taking.

"Our job is not to question another person's dream or to discourage them. It's quite the opposite. We must encourage them regardless of what it takes for them to chase their dreams and live them. That's what we do here: give hope and belief that people can follow their hearts. Max, every human being has the potential to become something extraordinary – they just need to search deep within to find what it is that excites them beyond all else."

Max was quiet for a moment. "I never realised this was what you were here for. Sounds silly really, because when I left here I was sure I would be the best violinist in the world. Others had said it before, but you cemented it for me."

"I'm glad we did, Max, but unfortunately, not everyone

takes our advice as wholeheartedly. So many people live their lives frightened by what's before them. They fear the challenge of taking risks, and they pass their fears on to their children. They fear life itself, frightened of getting it wrong, and so they play safe."

"I understand that," said Max, "but ultimately the kids will still do something in life, won't they?"

"Of course they will, but maybe not what they had dreamed of. Often they settle for second best because they are told to play safe."

"As someone who wanted to be number one at the violin, I couldn't have lived with second best."

"Exactly, Max. But this is what happens. The fear of failure prevents some parents encouraging their kids to embrace their dreams. They fear their child will fail and embarrass themselves and maybe even the family."

"I did face similar challenges," Max admitted. "My father didn't believe playing the violin held any value. He thought it was a waste of my time and wanted me to spend time doing other things. My mother believed I had something special in me when I played. Fortunately, so did my teacher. My father, however, fought hard to focus me on science subjects, which I didn't have a clue about and I honestly had no interest in either. It became the breaking point of our family, and my parents separated. Dad was so nice in every other way, but he couldn't seem to understand that violin was something a boy would want to do."

Tom spoke quietly. "So many families go through similar fights instead of welcoming new challenges or trying to excel at something."

Max nodded. "I think it's sad people can't aim high. There are so many things to do and achieve. There are thousands of places to visit and many different cultures to learn from. Why would people want to numb this out and essentially do nothing?"

"That's where we come in. We believe every person, adult or child has more to give than simply to survive life. We believe everyone can achieve something great. The best way we know to do this is to help people and encourage them. We tell them to believe in what they want."

"It's such a positive thing, believing in others," said Max.

"It is, and everyone should play their part and become a lighthouse keeper. We created this fantasy world of light and hope, telling youngsters we capture starlight in jars. They believe if they drink the secret potion, it will change their lives forever."

"It's true, though, isn't it?"

Tom and Maisie looked at Max. "It is if you believe it, Max. That's all you have to do: believe. It doesn't matter what you believe, Max, it only matters that you believe."

Max stared at them, stroking his chin.

"Ever since we arrived here, young people have come year after year, telling us what they want to be. We've heard it all: musicians, artists, dancers, doctors, architects and a thousand other professions. We've told every single person who's visited us that they're going to be great. Not good, but great. We know if you only give someone the right encouragement, they have the possibility of making it happen."

"I believed it."

"That's why you're successful, Max."

"And many other kids too. They drank their bottles believing they'd done something extraordinary. Some of them thought we had given them super-powers We would step back and say we saw a glow coming from them and they believed us. We sent every person away from here motivated for their future selves. They left with belief and hope that they would become the best at whatever they wanted to be. Over the years, many have come back to visit us. Look at these bottles, Max. So many of these kids made it to the top of their professions."

Max read the labels, hundreds of bottles each bearing a person's name, a date and a big red tick confirming a revisit many years after. There were many on the shelves without ticks. "What about these bottles here?"

"Works in progress, Max. Many more have still to return."

"For what reason do they come back?" asked Max.

"Usually for the same reasons you have today. They want to know what was in their bottle."

"And what was it?"

The lighthouse keepers stared at each other. They had been asked this many times, Max was sure. Maisie shuffled her feet and walked to where some fresh, glowing bottles sat. She held one up.

"Nothing, Max, just a harmless gas."

"What about the coloured light? My bottle was glowing red, and when I had finished it, the glow was gone."

Maisie laughed. "When Tom came up with this plan, he said it had to be one hundred per cent believable. Kids are smart and if they didn't believe totally, then the whole idea would never work. Before we moved here Tom's previous job was to put small ships into bottles, which were very popular. One day he showed me his magic. Using a small clear glass bottle with nothing in it, Tom filled it with his 'special gas'. Afterwards, it glowed green. I was so amazed."

"What was his secret?"

"A small Christmas tree lightbulb inside the bottle.

When he puts the gas inside, it turns on the light, glowing whatever colour of bulb is in the bottle. If it's red, he points the telescope towards Mars, or any old planet or star really. Most of the kids don't know one star from the next." Maisie looked at Tom questioningly. He nodded and she continued. "Tom always asks the kids what they want to be. He gets them to climb into the seat, and swing the telescope towards a star. If a child wants to be a romance author he might point his telescope at Venus, pick up an empty pink bottle, and attach it under the telescope. As Tom points it at the night sky, he presses a button to fill the bottle up with gas, which then turns on the light. The children believe the light comes from the star."

"Has it ever failed? Do the kids ever realise it's a trick?"

"No, never! They are mesmerised. To provide them with everything they need to be the best they can be, Tom explains how the light carries special powers. He emphasises how talented they are and how they can, and will, change the world. He always finishes it with the same phrase: "Believe that you can change the world for the better."

"That's what he said to me," Max said.

"And to all the others – and it works. As soon as they see the coloured bottle glowing in their hands, they believe there is magic in them. When they inhale the gas, the light disappears as if it is now part of them – ingenious. They all believe they have taken light beams from another planet. Which kid wouldn't be transformed by that?"

Max could see it all clearly; he remembered his night very well. "It certainly worked for me. Sometimes I felt low and didn't have enough faith in myself to get to the next level of my playing. It could be very depressing. I used to think back to my night here and believe I had something special within me. Now I realise it was your way of helping me dig deeper, a way of helping us realise our dreams. It worked. I believed you."

"Are you disappointed now that you know? Have we spoilt your dreams tonight?"

"No, of course not. It makes me slightly nervous now that I don't have the light from the bottle to help me when I perform." Max smiled. Now in his fifties, he realised this was strange to admit.

"But you never did have it. It was just a belief based on a harmless trick. Can't you see, the talent was always yours? We had nothing to do with your capability. We just helped you believe more in yourself to get you through the tough moments. It's what all parents and friends should do, help people to believe in themselves."

"I agree. I get it now, and I'm relieved. I came back to visit with expectations you both had magical powers and had come here from another world. I needed to find out what you had done to me. Now I realise I had it in myself. Your trick made me search out every last ounce of creativity I had to bring it out in my music. All I can do is thank you both. How can I repay you?"

The old couple smiled. They'd been asked this many times before.

"Send us people who have doubts or who have no belief in themselves, children or adults. If you do, we can help more people before the light in both of us is snuffed out. We'll hopefully help them become something, and not kill their spark like others may do."

Max nodded. "I'll send some people I know."

"Before you go, Max, we need you to sign the bottle you drank from."

"My bottle? You mean you still have it?"

"Of course. We have every bottle, from every person who ever dared to drink from it. Go back downstairs and find your bottle. It's about halfway down."

Max ran down the stairs and searched through the thousands of bottles of all shapes, sizes and colours. More names jumped out at him, famous people he knew, people from all walks of life he had come across or read about. As he climbed the stairs, he was fascinated by all the jobs and dreams that had been written on the bottles. At last his eyes fell on his bottle, his name clearly on the label. He picked it off the shelf and examined it. It didn't look anything special, and he was surprised that he remembered the details on the bottle exactly:

Max Bruford – 1977
World-Class Violinist

Underneath, in different writing, it read:

Purest light from Mars

Max smiled. He glanced at the bottle next to his, and his heart skipped a beat. It was Lily's.

Carefully, he took both bottles up the stairs, nervous he would drop either one. He handed his bottle to Maisie, who brought a large red felt pen out from her apron. She placed a large tick on the label and wrote 'success' on it. She passed it back to Max and asked him to sign it. He took a pen from his pocket, signed his name and dated it May 2018.

Max looked inside the bottle. He couldn't see any sign of a bulb. He asked Maisie where it was.

"We strip them out to put into the next bottles," she replied. "We believe in recycling."

"Where do you get all the bottles, are they expensive? There are some very nice ones."

"We never buy bottles. Most are washed onto the beach, some we find while walking and others have been donated to us. More recycling." Maisie smiled.

Max nodded. He was surprised at the number of bottles that could be washed up onto a beach. Then again this must have been over a period of many years, judging by the age of them.

Max handed Maisie Lily's bottle. "Do you know what happened to her?"

"Oh Lily, yes I remember her, nice girl, beautiful. Yes, she wanted love, Max, in particular, your love. Unfortunately for her, your determination and love of music was far greater than it was for her. She waited a while for you and then fell in love with a man when she was nineteen. She had three children, and they gave her all the love she needed. Later on, her husband abandoned her, and she's lived as a single mother most of her life. She followed your career closely and was tempted to contact you, but never did. She thought you wouldn't want to know someone with three kids."

Max stared in disbelief as Maisie rattled it off as if reading from a book. "How do you know all this?"

"We hear things."

"And she's never come back here again, her bottle sits unsigned?"

"That's true, although we know she will come back again. September thirteenth this year."

"What? How do you know this? Has she contacted you?"

"No, but we know she'll be here on that day."

Max took out his notebook and wrote down the date. He couldn't work out how they knew the things they did.

"Max, can you place Lily's bottle back where you found it? It's essential it goes back to the exact same spot. We don't usually allow people to handle another person's bottle."

"I'm sorry. I didn't realise." Max went back down the stairs and replaced both bottles on the shelf. He pushed them together so they were touching each other.

He sat with Tom and Maisie for the rest of the evening in the library quarters of the lighthouse. They drank tea and ate enormous meringues with fresh cream and strawberries.

They asked Max to play his violin once more, and he played the first movement, 'Reaching New Lands.' They were entranced with the beauty of the piece as it echoed up inside the building. His journey had come to an end. Forty years in the making and Max knew this day was as important to him for closure as his original visit had been.

He was packing away his violin when there was a loud knock at the door. Maisie was up out of her seat and almost ran down the stairs. She opened the door to three excited-looking children.

"Come in," she squealed, "how can we help you today?"

The first boy said the staff at Castle Toward had sent them.

"Up the stairs," Maisie said. "Pick an empty bottle you like from the crate at the bottom. You two can wait here for now."

The remaining children gawped at each other, wide-eyed, as their companion rifled through the crate.

The old couple looked at Max as they stood in the doorway. "You've done well," Maisie said and hugged him. "You've made us proud of what you have achieved. Keep playing and giving hope to other young players out there. Help people to believe in themselves, Max. Kids and adults, they need it."

Max nodded.

"One last thing. Don't be despondent when someone comes along who is better than you – it's part of the journey. Recognise their skill and be gracious. There will always be others better than us, that's progression."

Max nodded again. He had been given the title of world's most celebrated violinist many years earlier and often it felt like a burden to him. He'd be happy to pass the title on. "Thank you ... for everything."

The lighthouse keepers waved to him as he walked along the shore road, then turned back inside to entertain their latest young visitors.

21

THE NIGHT SKY

Max sat on the rocks, trying to process his visit. He had wanted this day for so long and was so glad the old man and woman were still alive to give him answers, although God knows how. They definitely must be both over a hundred years old, although that would have made them only in their sixties when he last saw them – not that much older than he was now. He felt a strange relief it was his own talent and not some magical light that had made him the musician he was.

The sun disappeared behind the darkened hills, the clouds fiery red against the powder blue sky. Stars appeared one by one, with only the brightest visible to the naked eye. The sky turned to the darkest blue it could be without turning black. As Max studied the night sky, he had a new idea for a piece of music; he could already hear it in his head as he looked upwards. He wrote 'The Night Sky' into his notebook. It was dark now with no light pollution from street lamps, and the sky became a blanket of stars. He had only ever seen the sky like this once before when he had cruised the Mediterranean.

He heard laughter coming from the top of the lighthouse and saw the silhouette of the old man pointing towards the stars. He pictured the young boy sitting legs astride the harness, holding on for dear life.

Max smiled; he'd been that boy forty years earlier. He remembered leaving with a cosy feeling of warmth, like being at home.

Max watched the beam of light sweep across the river; warning ships of the rocky coastline. He saw the old man take control of the light and point it towards the stars. It moved across the sky, searching through the darkness. Max grinned. The old man would be telling tall tales now, handing the boy a bottle filled with light. He watched as a blast of green light streamed down the lighthouse beam, filling the top of the lighthouse with a ghostly green glow.

Had he really just seen that? Hadn't he just been told that light didn't travel down towards the lighthouse? And thinking back, what about his balloons? Where was the bulb in them? He'd never seen any. A lot of this story still wasn't making any sense. Had they really told him everything?

Max saw the old man laugh as he held up a bottle that was glowing and pulsating the brightest green. He smiled. In many ways it didn't really matter what the truth was. If it helped these kids to believe in themselves, then why not? He knew when he had left here he believed he could do anything, which he would never have believed had he not visited the lighthouse.

The lamp spun around, searching the night sky for different stars, and Max saw the silhouette of another child climb into the chair. For the next hour, he could hear whoops and cheers coming from the lighthouse. Jars filled with light beams lit up the windows of the tower. Max watched as the kids inhaled their light.

Down below, another group of kids had gathered at the door. They must have heard what was going on and come down from the retreat. The door opened and the first children waved and disappeared off into the dark as the new ones entered. Max could hear their excited chatter carrying through the still of night.

He watched for a while longer until he saw the old couple hug and kiss; their evening's entertainment finished. All the lights went out except the main lamp, which continued sweeping in circles. Max walked back to his hotel, planning how he could return in September.

22

FINDING LILY

Once again, Max sat on the rocks watching the road to the lighthouse. It had been four months since his last visit but this time he had come for a different reason. Maisie had told him Lily would be revisiting on September thirteenth, and so here he was.

Max's palms were sweating and butterflies played havoc with his stomach. He was thankful it was so warm for September. He moved to a grassy verge and laid out his blanket. He wanted a clear view of the road to the lighthouse so he could check both cars and buses as they came along.

He tried to figure out if the lighthouse keepers actually knew if Lily was coming back today. He couldn't fathom how they knew such things and they weren't forthcoming with answers that made any sense to him. One thing he was sure of, everything they said had come true.

The small village of Toward was quiet. Max had only seen a handful of people in over four hours. He took his violin out and played 'The Night Sky', his new composition. But it didn't feel right playing it in broad daylight. He gazed at the water and tuned in to his surroundings, playing a song to nature. He captured the movement of a yacht and played to the fight it had with the wind, its sails full as it scudded along in the middle of the river. After lunch, he would revisit the lighthouse. Somehow he had a suspicion Tom and Maisie would already know he was here. He laughed to himself. He should have asked them what time Lily would arrive or if she had cancelled.

Two robins, fat as could be, fluttered on the ground, giving themselves a dust bath in front of where he sat. Max threw them some crumbs from his picnic. The robins were a good omen, as good things always seemed to happen to him when he saw one up close. Seeing two playing in front of him he was sure meant something special was about to happen.

He spotted another bus in the distance and gave a slight nod to the heavens to make this the one. His nerves were getting the better of him, his palms now sticking to his violin. This was the third bus of the day, and he had been at the side of the road for nearly five hours. Any locals watching him would be calling the police soon.

The bus stopped, and Max watched as three people got off and headed towards him. There wasn't much of a pavement for them to walk on – there was a choice of a grass verge or a walk on the road. The people were still too far away for him to recognise anyone. Two women walked at the front with their arms linked, and the third woman kept a slower pace behind them, hidden from view.

The strangest feeling came over Max. He could hear music, Lily's music – it was clearer than ever. He followed the melody he had played so many times. It became stronger as the women drew closer. The two in front appeared to be related, one young and one older. He still couldn't see the woman in the background, as her face was hidden by the other two.

The two women stopped in front of him, blocking his view as the other woman walked past. Max could only see the back of her head, but the music surrounding him was real. He was sure it was Lily: the feeling inside him was rising and the music coming at him like years before, it had to be her.

The young woman nudged the older one. "Is this what you mean by people here all come for the retreat?"

Max threw his violin into its case. In his haste to pack up quickly, he decided to leave his picnic where it was. He had to catch up and see if it was Lily. He was shaking uncontrollably.

"Would you like to play us a tune?" the older woman said.

Flustered, Max glanced up. "I'm sorry, I'm in a bit of a hurry. I need to catch up with someone."

The two women looked at the woman walking ahead. "Go catch your friend," said the younger of the two. There was something about her...

Max stared at the younger woman; it was like staring at Lily. It was her voice that caught his attention. The intonation, the dialect, her accent – if he closed his eyes, he was back forty years with Lily talking to him. He gazed at her in amazement, before looking at the woman beside her.

"Go on, Max, make me happy, play me my tune." Lily smiled the broadest smile imaginable. "Or are we keeping you from someone?"

Max glanced over at the other woman walking away and shook his head. Turning back, he saw the twinkle in Lily's eye. She still had a cheeky grin. She hadn't changed much and looked good for her age.

He couldn't speak.

"You're not going to run away from me again, Max Bruford, not after having waited this long to see you."

"Mum, what are you saying?" said the younger version of Lily. "Do you know this man?"

"Meet the one and only Max, honey."

"Mum, I think you're losing it." She turned to Max. "I'm sorry, sir, my mother is a little confused. She's thinking back to an old memory."

"I understand. Hopefully she'll be okay," said Max and smiled.

"Take that back, Max Bruford. You'll regret it if I tickle you."

"Mum! What are you saying?"

"It's Max, honey, here, live in person."

"Don't be silly, Mum, this can't be him. Why would he be sitting at the side of a road, in Scotland, in the middle of bloody nowhere, playing a violin?"

"Exactly. That's the question I'd like an answer to."

"Is it really possible that he's been sitting here, waiting for you to just happen by?" The younger woman stared at her mother intently. "Don't you think maybe you're just overwhelmed with the occasion of being back here? I knew this would be a bad idea."

"Hi Lily. I've missed you."

The younger woman spun round her, eyes fixed on Max. "Okay, now this is getting creepy. Is it me or am I losing my mind? Did you arrange this without telling me, Mum? Someone say something!"

Max smiled. "Like mother, like daughter. Are you as fiery as your mother?"

The younger woman ignored the question and stepped forward to get a closer look at him. "Can I ask, why are you sitting here, playing the violin? Are you teaching children at the castle?"

"No, nothing like that."

"So what are you doing here?"

"I was waiting for your mother. I heard she was coming back so I decided I couldn't let the opportunity pass. I had to be here."

"Rewind please, to the part where you said you found out she was coming back."

Max nodded. "That's correct. I travelled from London yesterday. It was a bit of a long shot, but I had to try and meet up with her again to explain things. Things that should've happened that didn't."

"Can we let the nostalgia trip go for now?" Puzzlement lined the younger woman's face. "I'm asking you how you knew. My mother didn't know herself until today she was coming here. So how could you possibly know?"

"She has a point, Max." Lily's voice was soft. "How did you know?"

"It's hard to explain. When you get to the lighthouse, you'll understand. Lily, you don't know what this means to me, meeting you again."

"I do, Max. I feel the same."

"All those letters we wrote to each other when we couldn't visit, which I still have, and then you turned up at my party with another guy – I was devastated."

"I know. You weren't to blame. I should've come back to you then. If I remember correctly, it was your nineteenth birthday. I had to stay with my boyfriend that night as he told me if I left him he couldn't go on living. I was in an awkward position and didn't want him to harm himself. After we left your place, he was so horrible to me. That evening I knew I should have left him, but couldn't. When the taxi dropped us off at the hotel we had a blazing row and he walked off. I asked the driver to take me back to your place but I couldn't find the courage to knock on your door again. I thought you weren't best pleased with me for being with him, so I went back to the hotel thinking I had lost two people in the space of one night. It's my biggest regret that I didn't leave him that night and come back to you."

"Mine too. I had always hoped we would get back together again."

"Excuse me," Lily's daughter interrupted. "Can you two stop talking like two fourteen-year-olds falling in love again? You don't know this man, Mum. You haven't seen him for forty years."

"That's where you are so wrong, my darling. I've never known anyone as intimately as I know Max. It sounds strange when all we ever had was ten days together, a few hundred love letters and a couple of planned meet-ups with our mothers present. But I can see he hasn't changed. Have you, Max?"

"I don't think so."

"Hold on, both of you. Stop talking and staring at each other. This is far more important. Mr Bruford – "

"Call me Max."

"Max. You couldn't possibly have known my mum was coming here. My mother didn't know herself until yesterday she was even coming to Scotland. I booked a bus trip to Inveraray, and this was her surprise, to visit the lighthouse. All she ever talked about was this bloody lighthouse and you. How could you possibly have known we were coming? I'm confused."

Max and Lily were only half listening. Lily leaned forward and kissed Max. "It's been too long, Max. What a wasted life for us. We should have been together."

Max found it hard to swallow as he struggled to control his emotions. The touch of her lips made him tremble. "I've wanted nothing else all my life, Lily. I would have traded the fame and accolades anytime to have had you, but stupidly I was on a mission to be the greatest."

"I know, Max, but I also couldn't walk away from the situation I was in. Realistically, I don't think I could've expected someone else to take on three kids from my failed marriage."

They wrapped their arms around each other and embraced.

Lily's daughter paced around them, working herself into a frenzy, unable to keep her thoughts to herself. "So this really is Max? Wonderful! Thanks, Mum, for naming me after a creepy guy who sits at the side of the road, waiting for you to walk off a bus. That's seriously sick."

"Have some manners, darling. This is my life-long friend."

"Hold on a minute." Max frowned. "I do not hang around roads, nor am I some creepy guy. I've only been to Scotland twice since I met your mother here. Once was in May this year for three days and the second time was just yesterday to arrive in time for her return. That's it."

"It still doesn't add up. I'm uncomfortable with this whole situation."

"What do you mean, named after me? In what way?"

"I'm Maxine, although Mum calls me Max. This was the closest my mother could get to remembering you, without telling my father."

Max shook his head and turned to Lily. "You called your daughter Max? What were you thinking?"

"I couldn't help it, it just happened. My husband wasn't that interested in what we called the children."

"I didn't know you felt that strongly about us! When you got married, I thought you genuinely didn't like me. When you stopped writing, I stuck to my music and tried not to think about you. Not so easy a task when one of my most famous songs is called 'First Love'."

"I guess not." Lily's face was a study. "Do you know how many times I've played *The Lighthouse Keepers* album? Thousands of times. Every time I hear my song, I feel the vibrations run through me. You captured me completely. My playfulness, my heart and my vulnerability. It's a masterclass in composition, Max. It's me through and through."

"That's the best compliment I've ever had. Thank you."

"She loves it," Maxine said. "I could never believe it was written for her. It's always played in our home."

"Haven't you loved anyone else, Max?" Lily asked.

"No, not really. I've had a few close friends, short-term relationships, but never anyone special. To be honest, I never wanted anyone else."

"Max, I feel dreadful you put your life on hold. We should've kept in touch."

"It doesn't matter now. What happened was for a reason. Tell me about your husband."

Lily sighed. She turned to her daughter, pleading with her eyes. "Maxine, would you mind giving us some space, love?"

Maxine snorted but did as her mother wished and moved away, pacing round in circles and kicking loose clods of earth up from the grass.

Lily turned back to Max. "My husband gave me three beautiful daughters, left and gave someone else a son. Which is what he always wanted. Each time I gave birth he was angry. 'Not another girl!' he would shout. We were only together for five years. All his talk of how he couldn't live without me, not quite so true. When I look back, I realise he only ever wanted me as a trophy. Someone to look after him, as he was chaotic. He never really loved me the way someone should be loved. He never let me talk, but lectured me on every subject. Every time I went to discuss something he would tell me what I really meant. I learned not to talk, to shut up and become a silent wife. No point talking except when he was out of the house and I could have fun with the girls. Sadly, for him, he missed everything I had to offer."

"I'm sorry to hear that."

"Don't be, I was better off without him. All I ever wanted was love. When I was young, I thought it meant love from a man, from you, Max. But over time I discovered it was the purest love I needed, and I got it from my three girls. Their love has made me happy. No matter the struggle, they give me everything."

"I'm glad you got what you asked for."

"Asked for?"

"Yes, in the lighthouse. You asked for a life full of love."

"And you asked to be the world's top violinist. I remember, you could see music."

"I still do. I saw it again as soon as you came off the bus. I'm thinking of writing 'Lily: the Return.'"

She grabbed his stomach, and he let out a yelp.

"What are you doing?" he said, laughing.

At the unexpected sound, Maxine could bear her banishment no longer and came running up. "She does it to my sisters and me all the time. She tickles us if she doesn't like an answer."

"I remember," said Max. "I would be laughing so much I cried, and your mum still wouldn't stop. It could be so painful. Your mum would climb on top of me and wouldn't let me go until she had her way."

"I'm not sure I want to hear the rest of this; it's beginning to sound gross. You didn't tell me this, Mum."

"There's a lot I didn't tell you."

"But back to Maxine's question, Max. How did you know I was coming here today?"

"When you get to the lighthouse it will become clear."

"I was expecting it to be gone by now."

"No, it's still there, and I think you'll love the owners, they are so nice."

"I remember the last ones, the old man and woman. They were so much fun, they helped me so much in life."

The three of them walked the remaining few hundred yards to the lighthouse. The sun shone through the trees, lighting up the leaves to bright lime green. Lily placed her hands on Max's shoulders, and he spun around.

"Magical memories, Max."

"On the coach, first day."

"That's right. As soon as I met you, life was different. Like we were meant to be together even at that young age. That's why I put my hands on your shoulders on the coach. I needed to touch you."

They arrived at the door of the lighthouse. It still looked the same.

"It's just as you described it, Mum, with the islands in the background and the Scottish hills. It's everything you said, except for the seals."

"Seals?" asked Max.

"Yes, the ones that swim in water."

Max laughed. He hammered the knocker against the door.

"What are you doing, Max, what will the owners think?"

"I'm sure they get it all the time, people returning to see the lighthouse."

"I suppose. It's guided me all through life, and now it's brought you back to me."

The door opened and Maisie stood there. "Hello Lily! Tom and I have been expecting you. And you, Max Bruford, we knew when we told you Lily was coming back, you too would return."

Lily stood, her mouth gaping wide.

"Come in and take a seat. It's lovely to see you again. Max, we'll call you in an hour if that's okay, we need to see Lily by herself, or with Maxine if she so wishes."

Maxine stared at the old woman. "How do you know my name?"

"Oh, I'm sure your mother or somebody mentioned it. Anyway, in you both come."

"I'll wait in the garden for you, Lily," said Max.

"Whatever you do, Maximus, do not leave."

Max smiled at the name she gave him. "I'm going nowhere, Lily-Anne."

She fired a look at him he remembered well.

Max walked to a corner of the garden and laid down his blanket. The sun was splitting the sky, and he thought about Lily and how beautiful she looked after all these years. Time hadn't diminished his love for her. He was surprised how young she looked. He picked a bunch of daisies, threading them through each other to make a necklace and bracelet. As he looked up at the top of the lighthouse, he saw Lily waving down to him.

He waved back.

His stomach was churning. Could this really be

happening? Since Lily got off the bus, he'd heard the most beautiful melodies in his head. Far more powerful and better than anything he had written in the past. He took out his notebook and wrote them down as he could see them. They were exquisite.

After what seemed an age, the door opened. Lily walked over to Max and sat down on his blanket. "Just like the old days, Max?"

"Better. Where's Maxine?"

"Talking to the lighthouse keepers. Can you believe they are still alive?"

"I know. The whole thing doesn't make any sense. Now do you understand how I knew you were coming?"

Lily nodded. "Although I still don't know how they know these things."

"I know, I find it all very weird. I think they are from another world or something; I can't find any reasonable explanation for any of this. Everything they say or do is as if they were with me just yesterday. Time doesn't seem to matter to them."

"I think you're right. And how could they possibly know Maxine's name? It doesn't add up."

Max handed Lily the daisy chain necklace, and she threaded it through her hair. "You look beautiful, Lily."

"Not so much now, Max. I've lost my best years, look at the wrinkles." She pulled at her face.

"I think you're perfect."

"Thank you, Max, it means a lot for you to say that, but honestly, you don't have to."

"I do, actually. The truth is the truth."

Lily smiled. "What are we to do? I'm so confused by today's events. When Maxine told me where we were going, I could picture you standing at the castle and the other places we'd been. And I arrive today, and here you are, in person. It's not what I was expecting – I'm still in shock."

"Me too. I came back here in May after forty years. I couldn't believe it when Tom and Maisie opened the door to the lighthouse. They knew I was coming and everything about me, my music career, the lot."

"Me too. They discussed my bottle and how I wanted love. Tom said I had achieved what I wanted. They said there was more to come, a lot more."

"What does that mean?"

"I don't know. What surprised me most was how they greeted me as if they had last seen me an hour earlier."

"I know, I was a bit freaked out by that. It beats me how they know these things, but they're always right."

"Do you think they'll tell us their secrets, how they know everything?"

"I don't think we'll ever know. Maybe we don't have to."

They heard a yell from the lighthouse. Max looked up and saw Maxine waving to them. From the ground, they couldn't see what was going on, but they both could imagine.

As they watched the light spin around, a few darts of coloured light headed towards the lantern of the lighthouse. They could hear Maxine shrieking with laughter.

"Big question, Lily."

"Oh, please don't. I'm not sure I can handle big questions. Can I?"

"Sorry, I didn't mean to scare you. Do you think in any way, there's a possibility we could think of getting together or at least keeping in touch?"

"Wouldn't I cramp your style, Max? You're used to the international stage and jet-setting across the world. I would've thought the last thing you needed was some boring housewife from a council estate in Carlisle holding you back."

"I agree." said Max. "When you put it that way it definitely sounds like a bad choice."

"You agree?" Lily looked hurt.

Max grabbed her and threw her back onto the blanket and looked into her eyes. "Yes, I agree with you, Lily. I don't want a boring housewife back in Carlisle. I want you and everything you have to offer. You're intelligent and witty, and we could have fun conversations into the early hours. I want a lover and a wife, someone that makes me happier than music. I want someone to sing songs with, go over lyrics, to dance and travel the world with me. I want you to make the next twenty, thirty, forty years, or whatever we have left of our lives, the best years – to live spontaneously. I need you, Lily, can you hear me? I need you."

Lily gazed at him, drinking in his every word.

"Lily, I love you like nothing else on this earth, and I want to show you off to the world. I want to lose myself in your body, every kiss, every caress, and I want you to be part of my life forever. The one thing I can honestly say is, you have never been boring."

She smiled at him, looking at his face. He was looking good for his age. He'd gained a few laughter and brow lines and his hair was a lovely silver colour. She knew she loved him but this was all such a shock.

"I want you too, Max. I always have, but we need to take time to get to know each other again. You may not like me as you did back then."

Max kissed her lips. His head couldn't handle the music and lights as their energy seemed to merge. They both felt the electricity they had years earlier. Just looking at each other was causing an unknown power to surge through their bodies.

"I love you, Max. Let's try again?"

Max stared at her with her crown of daisies and nodded. They kissed passionately, their hands caressing each other. Then Max tickled her and she screamed, breaking the spell. The world around them no longer mattered. Lily tried to tickle him back but he had the upper hand and she couldn't stop laughing.

The door of the lighthouse opened.

"Mum, what the hell are you doing? Stop it."

Tom and Maisie stood grinning in the doorway behind Maxine.

"I can hear wedding bells," Maisie called over.

"You can get married here," Tom added. "I'll run fairy lights all over the outside of the lighthouse."

"Max can organise a band!"

The old couple laughed.

Max and Lily stood up, rearranging their clothes and brushing themselves down.

"Mum, what the – "

"Shh, Maxine, it was only a bit of fun."

"A bit of fun? You were rolling around on top of each other. You need to act your age."

"Am I not supposed to say that to you, Maxine? It is okay to be in love at my age, you know. I'm not finished as a woman because I'm in my fifties; I still feel passionate and giggly and girlie and happy to do so. It's not a crime, is it?"

"Don't be ridiculous. You don't know him – you think you do, but you don't. You can't possibly be in love. As for passion in your fifties, that's disgusting."

"Maxine, when you're fifty you'll realise how alive you

still are inside. You see, inside I'm still fourteen. I've never grown up and never will."

"I give in. I'm trying to stop you making a fool of yourself."

"Don't you see? I want to be foolish. I want to grow old disgracefully, Maxine, that's where all the fun is. I think you need to understand something honey. From the day I met Max, I never stopped loving him. I may have married your father, and I did love him, but I never stopped loving Max in my head. He was always more important to me."

"If he was that important, why didn't you marry him instead?"

"Because I was pregnant with you. The last thing I wanted to be known as was the person who wrecked the family. So I stayed with your father."

"But you loved Dad, didn't you?"

"Yes, at one time. But I gave up what I really wanted for the sake of my children. Do you know how hard a struggle that's been for me all my life? Giving up the thing you really want and living in substitute mode?"

"You never said."

"I know. Your dad was hard work and awkward. When he said he was leaving I was concerned, obviously, having three kids, but the relief of him going was immense. In many ways, I was happier to live by myself than stay with someone who treated me as he did."

"It's all a bit too much for me to hear this, Mum."

"I know, honey, but do one thing for me."

"What?"

"Listen to the song that Max wrote for me. It's the truest reflection of what Max and I felt, what we were back then. Max and I know each other better than anyone else could ever fathom. It may only have been a short time we were together, but it was an intense, deeply emotional connection we made for life. I would say it was spiritual and the connection has never been broken."

Max nodded. "It's true, Maxine. Every word."

"I don't want my mum hurt," Maxine said, her eyes imploring Max. "She is used to living by herself and is content with what she has."

"Do you like your mother living alone?"

"She doesn't mind; she's used to it."

"You've never asked me that question, Maxine.'

"Well, do you mind?"

"There's not many things worse in life than living alone, honey. It's a terribly lonely life, going back to an empty house. I have no one to talk to, and when there's good news like your sister having a baby, there's no one to celebrate with. Locking up at night is unsettling. The worst part is when I'm feeling poorly, lying day after day with no one coming through the door. I hate it. Very few people like living alone. They may put on a brave face to the outside world but deep down most people would rather be with a partner, someone to share things with."

"Oh Mum! You've never said any of this before."

"You've got your own life to lead, Maxine, I'm not here to tell you my issues."

Maxine hugged her mum. "I'm so sorry I never realised."

"It's okay. I'm fine. All I want is for you to trust any decisions I make regarding myself and Max."

Maxine looked at Max. "Promise me you won't ever hurt my mother."

"I promise I can only make your mother happy. We've hurt each other enough. All we want is to be together."

"How will I know you really love her?"

"Why do you think I'm here today? Why did I cancel some of my music engagements to sit here at the side of the road, waiting on your mother to walk past?"

"Maxine, forget about Max and me. Tell me, did you like being inside the lighthouse with Tom and Maisie?"

"It was unbelievable, Mum, you should see inside and what happens. Could you see me on the harness from here?" She looked up and realised they couldn't. "Tom gave me a shot in the harness, and it was amazing, even in daylight. The lamp can track the stars and catch light from them. I'm coming back tonight at eleven once all the kids are finished and I'm getting my own bottle to fill with light. Maisie said it's better doing it in the dark."

"That's good. Make sure you think clearly about what you ask for in life. Don't make any rash decisions or the mistake I made."

"I know; I need to be very clear about what I want to be."

"I thought you didn't believe in all this catching light from the stars, Maxine." Lily smiled at her daughter. "You said what I had told you about the lighthouse was all fairy stories."

"Well, I believe it now I'm here and can see it for myself. I saw your bottle and Max's sitting next to each other on the shelf, even after forty years."

"That's what I've been telling you, how important the lighthouse has been to us. I've just realised, you can't come back tonight, Maxine. We need to be back to meet our bus at the hotel in Inveraray."

"Forget about the bus tour, Mum, I'll call them. This is far more exciting. I need to find us a hotel."

"There's room at the one I'm in," said Max. "I'll call them."

"This place is so incredible, Mum. I don't want to leave."

"I'm afraid it's back to work on Monday, Maxine."

"It doesn't have to be," said Max. "Let's take a holiday for the next week and talk some things over. You wouldn't need to work again if you wanted."

"What kind of woman do you think I am, Max Bruford? Of course I need to work. I'm not going to be a kept woman."

The old man was clearing his throat, trying to get their attention. He and Maisie stood in the doorway of the lighthouse.

"Sorry Tom, we got carried away with our domestic issues."

"That's okay, son. It's getting late, and we need to get ready for our young visitors tonight. There's a new batch of kids up at the castle, so we need to be organised."

"Of course, Tom. Thank you both for another amazing day. We're heading back to the hotel. We'll come and say goodbye tomorrow if that's okay?"

"Ideal. Come at midday, and we'll have a sandwich."

They said their goodbyes.

"I'll be back tonight," said Maxine. "See you then."

As the lighthouse keepers turned to go back inside, Tom called over his shoulder, "Will we get an invite to the wedding?"

"Jeez, we've only just met! Let's stop talking about weddings. We never said we were getting married."

"I can tell you the date if you want," said Maisie.

They all stopped in their tracks.

"You don't know that," said Max, looking at Lily. "You can't. You're making it up."

"I'm not. It's the twenty-fifth of June."

"No!" They all said together.

"Max, can I ask you a question to think over tonight?" said Tom.

"Sure, Tom, what can I do for you?"

"Would you and Lily consider – not now but sometime in the future when you retire – running the lighthouse for us? Think about it, son. You don't have to make your mind up now: sometimes in the next couple of years would be good. We can talk about it tomorrow." He took Maisie's hand, and they disappeared into the cottage again.

"Run the lighthouse, Max. Did he really say that? Imagine living here next to the water. Wouldn't that be the ultimate job, giving people hope?" said Lily, her eyes shining.

"I'm in shock. I can't believe he asked us that."

The sun had slipped behind the hills and darkness fell quickly. Max called the hotel and asked them to book another room and send a taxi.

As they started to walk down the road, the three of them hand in hand, Max pointed to the rocks.

"Look, Lily, a family of seals."

"It must be an omen." She hugged him "I love you, Maximilian, and I'm not letting you go, ever again."

"Whoa. Stop right there, Lily-Anne. How did you ever find out my real name?"

"On one of the hundred interviews I've followed you on, maybe *Desert Island Discs*."

"Oh, I didn't realise I had mentioned it. Do you still want to date a guy with the name Maximilian?"

"I could live with that."

"Well, why don't you make me the happiest man alive then and marry me?"

They stood cheek to cheek, a single tear escaping Lily's wide eyes as she nodded her reply.

Maxine looked at her mother, and could see how happy she was. She wrapped her arms around both of them. "Looks like the twenty-fifth of June may be on then. Can I join in the hug, it's kinda lonely out here?"

Max and Lily put their arms around Maxine.

They stood waiting at the side of the road. Max started to hum Lily's tune and soon the other two joined in, each of them humming different parts, gently rocking back and forth. As they sang louder they started to dance, the three of them in a circle. Had anyone been passing, they would have wondered at the sight of three adults waltzing back and forth, singing at the top of their voices in the dark.

The lights from the taxi lit up the road and stopped before them.

A LITTLE BIT OF HELP

Can you help me, please?

If you've enjoyed this book, I would appreciate your help. The best way to help an aspiring author like me is straightforward – to give my book a review.

I don't have a large following, and so every review is like gold dust. I'm not in any way asking you to write a fantastic review, just an honest account of what you thought of *The Lighthouse Keepers*. Fair reviews can bring this book to the attention of other, like-minded readers and hopefully they, too, will enjoy the book.

Leaving a review will only take a few minutes of your time and you can do so wherever you purchased this book. You can generally find me by searching Grahame Anderson The Lighthouse Keeper.

Thank you in advance and please look out for my future publications – I have many stories still to tell.

ABOUT THE AUTHOR

Grahame Anderson is the author of *The Lighthouse Keepers*, Short Stories and Poems Vol. 1, and *The Best Seat in the Universe*.

You can visit him at
www.grahameanderson.co.uk

Email: info@grahameanderson.com

Grahame lives with his wife, Brenda, and two sons in the small town on the West Coast of Scotland. He has been involved in print and media for over forty years. When not writing, Grahame will be listening to music or reading books.

facebook.com/GrahameAnderson
instagram.com/grahameanderson

THANKS

Writing a book is rarely a solo act. So many people in their own way helped me complete this book.

* * *

Thanks to Brenda, Luke and Roan for the encouragement and belief in me and giving me the space to dream my dream over the past two years.

Also to Tommy, Brian, Mena, Fiona, Harry, the members of Greenock Writers' Club and the skilful editing by Bryony Sutherland.

To everyone else who commented and gave support especially the members of the Self Publishing Formula Community on Facebook for direction on my cover artwork.

THE BEST SEAT IN THE UNIVERSE

Worrying about your direction in life?

Discover a simple method to guide you to a better future.

Feeling stuck and lacking momentum? Not completely sure who you are? Author and business owner, Grahame Anderson, shares his unique approach to unleashing your insecurities with a powerful story that reveals the profound simplicity of helping you take steps to reset your life.

The Best Seat in the Universe is a story-based journey centred around a young man and his grandad, as they embark on a behind-the-scenes look at life in search of The Best Seat in the Universe. Their quest is built upon the metaphor of a bus journey from birth till death and everything in between. By crystallizing your purpose and direction, you'll soon be filled with the energy and clarity to make you ready to take on the challenge to a better life.

In *The Best Seat in the Universe*, you'll discover:

- A clever and thoughtful way to help you find your unique trail to blaze
- Insights into how to free yourself from the control of others and regain life's balance
- Ways to move past failure and automatically let every so-called mistake lead you to accomplishment
- The keys to taking charge of yourself and following the best route to happiness
- Simple steps to unveil your perfect plan, inspirational moments, and much more.

The Best Seat in the Universe is a life-changing guide to help you pave your way. If you like motivating messages, thought-provoking concepts and practical approaches, then you'll love this modern-day story.

Read *The Best Seat in the Universe* and put yourself firmly in the driver's seat, heading towards your true destiny.

Printed in Great Britain
by Amazon

85659290R00116